BLACKS AND BRITANNITY

For Jean-Claude and Nicolas

Blacks and Britannity

DANIÈLE JOLY

With a contribution by Cathie Lloyd and David Owen

Ashgate

Aldershot • Burlington USA • Singapore • Sydney

Published by
Ashgate Publishing Limited
Gower House
Croft Road
Aldershot
Hampshire GU11 3HR
England

Ashgate Publishing Company
131 Main Street
Burlington, VT 05401-5600 USA

Ashgate website: http://www.ashgate.com

British Library Cataloguing in Publication Data
Joly, Danièle
   Blacks and britannity
   1. Minorities - Great Britain 2. Minorities - Great Britain -
   Social conditions
   I. Title
   305.8'00941

Library of Congress Control Number: 2001095452

ISBN 0 7546 1149 3

Contents

List of Figures

List of Tables

Acknowledgements

All my thanks go first to Michel Wieviorka, Director of the Centre d'Action et d'Intervention Sociologique (Paris), who invited me to join his team for an innovative and stimulating research experience. He also made it possible for sociological intervention to be carried out in Britain for the first time. I would like to thank those who in Birmingham contributed to the sociological intervention sessions; my main team members Denise Amory and Eric Mace and also Olivier Cousin, Khursheed Wadia and Lynnette Kelly and above all, all the young people who took part in it. Many thanks also to our interlocutors.

We owe the funding for this piece of research to the RATP (Réseau Autonome des Transports Parisiens). As ever Rose Goodwin meticulously prepared the text for publication.

My warmest thanks finally go to my friend John who has been enormously supportive and caring. John Rex and his immense knowledge have inspired much of my thinking throughout my research work.

Preface

Michel Wieviorka

What is the utility of social sciences? For some researchers, social sciences constitute learning in their own right, a body of knowledge based on various requirements of stringency and reliability, which form the basis of the organisation of academic discussion and professional life in academic journals, in symposiums or, quite simply, within the university, which may well remain isolated from the general life of the city. For others, and sometimes also for the same, social sciences provide the tools, knowledge and know-how required by decision-makers, or those who challenge them: political actors, heads of firms, or trade-unions for example. They are a form of technical expertise and are the basis of advisory functions.

Other researchers, on the contrary, far from these orientations, consider that the task of the social sciences is primarily to provide a critical point of view. Here, the aim of the knowledge they produce is to provide material not for professional circles, but for public discussion, preferably in highly critical terms – a process which does not necessarily involve any relationship, even a strained one, with any actor whatsoever. In this situation the researcher is politically involved, his or her profile is that of the intellectual, of which he or she is one example among many. From this point of view, he or she may be an organic intellectual, in the service of an actor who is dominated or challenged; or yet again, he or she may be very different, claiming to be totally uninvolved and purely critical in attitude.

It is obvious that the book which Danièle Joly has just completed does not fit either of these descriptions. Or, rather, it borrows the best of both, leading to an approach of which the originality deserves to be stressed – I will do so later. The contents, particularly the first four chapters of the book, are in the first instance a fundamental and well-argued contribution to what constitutes one of the major discussions of our era: the question of cultural difference, its nature, and the policies elaborated to deal with it in political terms. Thus, with the collaboration of Cathie Lloyd, Danièle Joly has assessed the knowledge available on ethnic relations in Great Britain, the country in Europe which found the way to analyse and scientifically discuss this question long before the others Danièle Joly then discusses the concept of ethnicity and other related themes, contextualising them in particular in relation to the concepts of hybridization and creolisation; she has reconstructed the political question of ethnic minorities and of immigration and given the researcher David Owen the possibility of presenting a sensitive and illuminating monograph on the specific case of the city of Birmingham. All this puts Danièle Joly's work at the highest level in academic discussions on ethnicity, minorities, immigration, etc. At the same time, the social and political criticism reveals Danièl〉 Joly's central preoccupation: the desire to convey the experience of young people of Afro-Caribbean origin in Great Britain – an experience which is a combination of contempt, racist rejection and social exclusion.

But Danièle Joly goes much further and the above remarks are only preparing the way leading to the main point. Hers is an account of a social and cultural problem which reveals aspects our society too often refuses to consider, and therefore articulates a highly rigorous approach with a critical position. But it does not stop there. Danièle Joly reveals the oppression, the prejudice, the particularly unfair treatment which the Black Caribbean origin youths meet; but she also lets them speak and enables them to produce their own analysis of their situation and to consider the conditions necessary for them to carry out actions likely to transform this situation.

Her sociology then becomes, for the first time in Great Britain, that of sociological intervention. Here the researchers go further than simply allowing those they study to speak – though this is itself a step forward. They set up a means of co-producing knowledge, and invite the actors to join them in thinking about their action. The method of the sociological intervention is based on the establishment of an intense and demanding relationship between the researchers, who elaborate hypotheses and submit them to the actors and the latter, who discuss these hypotheses, appropriate them if they seem to fit or elaborate new ones with the researchers if they do not.

In other approaches, research findings are based on documents or on the analysis of taped interviews – which Danièle Joly knows how to do very well – without the people concerned having their say; at the most, the researchers occasionally present the results of their analysis to the actors for their information – a restitution as a mark of their appreciation. But in the sociological intervention methodology, the findings are primarily the outcome of the relationship between the actors and the researchers – one might almost say the test or the demonstration of this inter-relationship. For once, the actors participate in the production of the knowledge concerning them, they are the *subjects* of the research and not the *objects*. I am certain that the reader will benefit immensely from the last chapters in which young people of Afro-Caribbean origin, in the course of several meetings with the different people invited to participate, then directly with the researchers, co-produce the auto-analysis of their own situation – and the possibilities of dealing with them. I am sure, too, that he or she will find many surprising elements in this auto-analysis, which proves to be often contrary to what is generally expected.

The reader will permit me a few more personal remarks. This research, as Danièle Joly reminds us, has been carried out in the context of a programme which I initiated and which aimed at a better understanding, particularly in France, of the links between urban violence, feelings of insecurity, social inequality and cultural difference. Danièle Joly is part of this research because there have been intellectual links between the centre which she directs today and the CADIS for several years. A close Franco-British cooperation has been developed here in which several researchers, on both sides of the Channel, have joined forces to elaborate hypotheses together, carry out fieldwork, think about the way to deal with their findings, while each research team has retained considerable autonomy in its publications. This is an experience which, in my opinion, is exemplary – and which I hope will be the basis for closer relations between researchers in the two countries.

Introduction[1]

Danièle Joly

This research started as part of a collaborative project launched and coordinated by Michel Wieviorka (CADIS) in Paris. It proposed to study urban violence and insecurity in a number of cities in Europe, focusing on difficult areas of the *banlieues* and the inner cities. I was in charge of the British leg of the project and I selected Birmingham as a suitable site for the empirical work for two main reasons: being a large industrial conurbation with a multicultural population, it is a representative site for Britain and in addition we could take advantage of a good body of research on Birmingham carried out by colleagues including myself at the Centre for Research in Ethnic Relations (CRER). I then proceeded to establish a brief overview of 'violence', the populations concerned and the responses by public bodies in Birmingham, according to the parameters defined for the broader project (Wieviorka et al. 1999). The general picture emanating from this initial sketch is that Birmingham remains a moderate city with a relatively low level of violent incidents in the 1990s (see Appendix I).

However, feelings and perceptions of insecurity are not necessarily commensurate with the level of crime and violent incidents. In Birmingham, thus, a number of centrally funded or local authority based initiatives propose to deal with the issue of violence, mostly targeting inner-city areas. To an extent such programmes may unintentionally contribute to the perception that those constitute dangerous neighbourhoods. In addition, the media and public opinion tend to pin 'violence' onto young African-Caribbean males as though they had a near monopoly of it. Generally the media are unequivocal in the image of crime and violence which they project and which influences public opinion: they home in on young African-Caribbean males as the epitome of aggression, mugging, drug trafficking, rioting, general crime and delinquency. This stereotype relentlessly surrounds the group concerned and categorises it. They are at the receiving end of much racism and discrimination as confirmed by the MacPherson report (1999). This led us to concentrate on this population in the British project. An additional dimension had to be taken into account: the fact that British society makes an institutional space for ethnic groups and formally implements ethnic monitoring and multicultural policies. As a consequence the question of ethnicity is placed on the agenda alongside those of racism and discrimination. What we were concerned with was the positioning of the young people within this context and in particular with the formulation of group identification and action. Theoretically, we drew on the interaction between categorisation and self-definition as developed *inter alia* by Jenkins (1998), on concepts of alienation and resistance, social networks and on the CADIS work in the area of social movements. Methodologically, sociological intervention was particularly appropriate as we concentrated on the young people themselves.

The methodology adopted was that of sociological intervention as developed by Alain Touraine (see Chapter Five) and the group selected was composed of young African-Caribbeans whose parents were immigrants from the Caribbean islands but who themselves had grown up in Britain. This was complemented by the research already carried out by myself and colleagues at CRER, published literature, qualitative fieldwork in Birmingham among members of ethnic groups, policy-makers and practitioners, and the analysis of relevant statistics. In this study our attention focused on the young people themselves who were at the same time presumed victims and perpetrators of violence. We aimed to find out their relationship to this violence, its meaning, how they were affected by it, fell into it and possibly overcame it; how they constituted themselves as social actors and subjects, and what was their experience and capacity for action. The main questions asked regarding the group selected, were set within a theoretical framework drawn from research on racism and ethnic groups. What the data yielded was that violence was not the main issue motivating the important questions to be asked. To phrase it in an oversimplification and even according to the young people, it was not their problem, it was society's problem. Questions on it had been answered; the group had progressed beyond. It was clear to them that the symbolic violence constituted by racial discrimination accompanied and affected all aspects of their lives; it was overarching and manifested itself acutely in encounters with the police and the judiciary. They also explained how racism and social deprivation, compounded with their sequels, had led some of them into petty crime and delinquency. In their view the important questions to be asked were those of group identification, resources of action, how to overcome handicaps, and how to enhance their capacity for action, and these coincided with the main thrust of our research framework.

The book is organised into the following chapters. Chapter One presents the history and the state of the art in immigration and ethnic relations research in Britain. Cathie Lloyd took the lead in writing this co-authored chapter. Chapter Two examines ethnic minorities and settlement from a theoretical viewpoint. Chapter Three gives an overview of ethnic minorities and policies in the UK in the post-World War II period. Chapter Four, written by David Owen, analyses key statistics concerning ethnic minorities and related issues in Birmingham. Chapter Five looks at the make-up of Blacks within British society. Chapter Six examines the meanings and capacity for action.

Note

1 The terms used for the group which is the main protagonist in this book have changed: they were usually called West Indians in the initial period of settlement in Britain, the term Black became prevalent in the end of the 1970s to be followed in the 1980s by Afro-Caribbean, and more recently African-Caribbean (following usage in the USA).

  Britannity is a novel way to express 'pertaining to Britain' without pre-empting a specific interpretation attached to it.

Chapter One

Research in Ethnic Relations in Great Britain: State of the Art Today

Cathie Lloyd and Danièle Joly

Introduction

British research in the area of ethnic relations has been profoundly affected by the fundamental changes which have been taking place in the world over the past 20 years and which have created a climate of great uncertainty. While the impact of membership of the European Union has generated considerable debate, wider issues have also been salient. We have seen how the collapse of communism in Eastern Europe has given rise to new foci of conflict. The war in the Balkans shows that we can no longer make comfortable assumptions about economic, political and social structures or their capacity to contain conflict or integrate newcomers. Governments throughout the world have been introducing new restrictions on immigration and asylum policy at the same time as a disturbing rise of ethnic nationalism, racial violence and the extreme right (Ford 1992). These developments have had an impact on the lives of settled ethnic minority populations. Proponents of the theory of 'globalisation' stress that national governments can make little impact on their own on this state of affairs although closed formulations of this idea are strongly contested by writers who dispute the novelty of these developments and argue that there are new ways in which democratic influence can be brought to bear (Hirst and Thompson 1996). Others point to the way in which the cultural arena is increasingly characterised by syncretism and global influences, so that youth culture is both international and profoundly local/tribal (Back 1995; G. Bauman 1997; Hall and du Gay 1996).

How has British research on ethnic relations responded to these bewildering changes? In this chapter we briefly review the British approach to immigration and the 'tradition' of research on ethnic relations in Britain since the 1950s, and then consider recent continuities and discontinuities in this subject area from the 1980s.

The Background and British Immigration Policy

Research on ethnic relations in Great Britain has been shaped by a number of influences. Firstly, our understanding of post-war migration was within the context of the plural entity which makes up the United Kingdom, with minority languages in Wales and (more isolated) parts of Scotland and Northern Ireland. Secondly, the British have been strongly influenced by the research tradition of the USA. A 'common language', political links and the heritage of African-Caribbean communities mean that publications become available quickly and exchanges enable new ideas to cross the Atlantic rapidly. This influence has until recently helped to sustain an understanding of ethnic relations in terms of a dichotomy between Black and white members of society and stress the 'colour' or 'race' question both in social interaction and in sociological studies. The third influence is British immigration policy, which took place in the context of decolonisation and was framed in terms of theories of 'race relations' (Rudder and Goodwin 1993). The idea of 'racism' as a problem within British society, rather than a problem caused by immigration, entered the debate largely in the 1970s (Dummett 1973; Moore 1975; Sivanandan 1982).

Post-war immigrants came to Britain mainly from its ex-colonies in South Asia (India, Pakistan and later, Bangladesh) and the Caribbean, although at different periods people also came from West Africa, Vietnam, Hong Kong, Taiwan and Cyprus. Migration from Ireland has been a constant (Hickman and Walter 1997; Lloyd 1995). Immigrants from the New Commonwealth were British citizens and not, initially, subject to immigration control. However, Britain was the first country in Europe to move to control immigration, gradually through a system of quotas (1962) and then in reaction to the flight of Asians from Kenya and Uganda in 1968 and 1972; their rights to enter the country were restricted. Rights of entry are determined by citizenship which falls into three categories with diminishing rights (full British citizens, citizens of dependent territories and overseas British citizens) according to the 1981 Act effective from 1983.

The United Kingdom is not a signatory of the Schengen agreements and British governments have consistently opposed the extension of European Union powers in the domain of immigration. This rationale is based on Britain's geographical situation as (a collection of) islands but also on a rather censorious attitude towards the ability of other Europeans to control immigration. Another argument sometimes advanced is that internal controls would not be possible here as the British are not expected to carry identity cards, but this does not prevent raids on suspected illegal immigrants or police checks on Black people.

Opposition to the idea of a European common immigration policy has not prevented British governments from enacting most of the control measures common in other countries and sometimes pre-empting EU policies, such as the Carriers Liabilities Act, the requirement of visas for entry and restrictions on asylum. Immigration is not a controversial issue for the two main political parties, rather, there is a remarkable bipartisan consensus about immigration underscored by Labour's conservatism when in office (Layton-Henry 1992, p. 155).

The British nationality law of 1981 is a patchwork which combines the *jus sanguinis* with the *jus soli*, although the introduction of the 'patriality' clause has shifted the balance towards *jus sanguinis*. Immigrants born overseas become eligible to apply for British nationality after 10 years of uninterrupted residence. In Britain there an important distinction between civic rights and nationality. Commonwealth residents and Irish nationals in Britain have had civic rights (to vote, to stand for office, to form associations) irrespective of their nationality. The question of rights helps to explain why the term 'immigrant' is not used any longer for settled residents in Britain. The early introduction of migration controls and the disturbances in Notting Hill and Nottingham in 1958, gave rise to a considerable research interest in the subject of migrants in British cities.

We will now give a brief overview of this early research on ethnic relations in Britain since the 1950s, as it is essential to understand this history in order to appreciate the broad traditions from which contemporary writers have emerged.

A Brief Retrospective: Research in Britain the 1950s, 1960s and 1970s

Research in the 1950s was dominated by what was seen as the 'novelty' of post-war immigration, although it is now well established that migration has been an integral part of British history (Merriman (ed.) 1993). Research focused mainly on migrants' settlement in urban areas and their relations with the 'white' British. The new area of sociology/social policy research on ethnic minorities was strongly influenced by the existing British traditions of ethnography and quantitative survey work and a continuing tradition of empirical and positivist research (Rex 1961).

The new ethnic minority populations were measured in almost every conceivable way in a series of survey-based studies at the (old) Institute of Race Relations which conceived ethnic relations in terms of a social problem subject to a process of adjustment in which prejudice would be gradually eradicated (Bourne 1980; Rose and Deakin 1969; Deakin 1970). This work was continued by the independent Policy Studies Institute (PSI) which conducted a survey entitled 'Black and White Britain', which set the agenda for the work of the Commission for Racial Equality set up under the Race Relations Act 1976 (Daniel 1968; Smith 1974). It was widely assumed that British society was basically tolerant and that the problem of 'race relations' had been imported from the colonies from which immigrants had come.

From the 1970s, criticism of the approach which tended to present immigrants as a social problem, argued that there were serious problems of racism to be confronted in British society and, influenced by Black Power and anti-colonial discourses, challenged the role of white sociologists as the sole interpreters of ethnic relations (Bourne 1980; Dummett 1973; Hiro 1971; Moore 1975).

Sociological research from the late 1960s attempted to take the theoretical aspects of our subject further, producing what has become known as the race relations 'paradigm'. On the one hand were the cultural pluralists who argued that contact and proximity would in time improve 'race relations' (Banton 1967; Patterson 1968). Proponents of this approach argued that ethnicity was flexible and adapted to changing contexts while anthropologists tended to portray immigrants' economic choices as determined by their cultural backgrounds (Wallman 1979; Watson 1977). For John Rex on the other hand, the key elements of study was the way in which the 'race relations situation' was determined. He was interested in the way a group of people could be defined as different and exploited or oppressed as such. Focusing on questions of power, status and stratification, Rex studied discrimination in the provision of scarce resources, notably in the housing market, and showed how ethnic minorities were systematically disadvantaged and maintained in an 'underclass' position (Rex 1967). In a second phase, his studies of ethnic associations and mobilisation strengthened the notion that ethnic minorities were not passive subjects of social processes but active social actors (Rex 1970, 1979; Rex, Joly and Wilpert 1987).

This work was one important influence on the understanding of how discrimination operates in society. Another was that of the movement for equal opportunities for women which led to the enactment of an Equal Pay Act in 1973 containing the concept of 'indirect discrimination' developed in the USA (Sooben 1990). It seemed easier to intervene effectively against such indirect and institutional discrimination, so for the purposes of public policy they have largely replaced the emphasis on individual prejudice. As Sivanandan commented, what was important was the use of power and the 'acting out' of discrimination (Sivanandan 1982).

The idea of indirect discrimination became a key element of the new race relations law introduced in 1976 which in turn helped to determine much of the empirical research which sought to test the existence of discrimination. While research on immigration control procedures ended in a court ruling which debarred the Commission from intervening in that area in future (CRE 1984a) other work highlighted modes of discrimination in the provision of public housing in working class areas (CRE 1984b and c). A meticulous study of recruitment procedures in a London medical school revealed how discrimination was built into the computerised processing of applications (CRE 1988). The CRE also carried out periodic reviews of the operation of the legislation (CRE 1992, 1985).

At the end of the 1970s a number of key items were emerging onto the research agenda. The new CRE required research to help it begin its work on tackling racial discrimination, and part of this was to be through pressure for an ethnic group question in the census which was finally achieved in 1991. This was surrounded by divided views and controversies among sociologists, some of whom opposed the census question. A growing body of criticism of earlier concepts of 'race' and ethnic group, argued that these ideas should be situated within a broader sociopolitical perspective. The outline of this research was set out by the work of the Centre for Contemporary Cultural Research, which focused on the relationship between the criminalisation of young people and the development of an authoritarian state, 'the law and order society' (Hall et al. 1978; Scarman 1981). Ethnic relations were also to be theorised in the context of cultural studies (CCCS 1982).

A good deal of this new literature was dedicated to the study of the 'riots' which shook several British towns in 1980, 1981 and 1985. Researchers, practitioners and politicians have paid attention to this theme. The different interpretations proposed to account for these events can be summarised as follows.

One group of explanations was based on a functionalist structuralist approach which more or less corresponded to the Conservative Party discourse. According to this view, existing structures were adequate and the riots were the results of an aberration which derived from irresponsible elements: either foreign elements, extremists, troublemakers, agitators or delinquents pertaining to a phenomenon of deviance commented by Benyon and Solomos (1987). Another explanation was that of imitations, copycat riots, another influence from without. The social processes put forward to explain these phenomena are the following as criticised by Hazel and Carby (1982): a deviant form of family with the normal traditional family being replaced by single mothers, the Caribbean matriarchate or an excessive Asian patriarchate. Social disorder was seen as resulting from the upheaval in communities, caused by the arrival of new populations, in particular immigrants. Moral degeneration, lack of respect for the law, decadent values were perceived to derive from the collapse of institutions which traditionally imparted social control (school, family etc.). The 'lack of culture' was also indicted; Caribbean culture was not deemed to be sufficiently developed (Pryce quoted by Lawrence, 1982). Ethnic minority youths were categorised as rootless or caught between two cultures. Finally, problems associated with ethnic minority communities came under the remit of the police as a question of social control in the narrowest sense of the term, i.e., purely a police problem, a construction analysed by Gilroy (1982).

Within a broad Marxist framework, riots were considered as the logical consequence and an expression of the class struggle: 'old fashioned class war' brings about 'old fashioned riots' (Pearson, 1983), the reproduction of the under-proletariat constituting the material foundation of this phenomenon accompanied by alienation. It was argued that young people who participated in the riots had no voice and were completely marginalised politically; they were victims of the crisis of capitalism and its concomitants (Pearson, 1983). Unemployment, unsatisfactory housing, poverty, social disadvantage, insufficient facilities for young people, all the indices of poverty were present (Scarman, 1981). Those youths belong to classes which are considered dangerous by the ruling class, dangerous classes in dangerous areas (Body-Gendrot 1995). Margaret Thatcher expresses clearly this viewpoint, equating muggers, strikers and rioters as 'the enemy within' (quoted by Gilroy, 1982). They were one of the main targets of the repressive state apparatus, in particular the police. As a conclusion, riots were perceived as a legitimate means to support a claim for the redistribution of power and resources. According to this approach, riots have the significance of a rational and instrumental action.

However, additional approaches complement the above by arguing that exploitation, poverty, unemployment and social disadvantage are necessary but insufficient factors to explain the riots. Other processes have to be taken into account. More than social disadvantage, it is racial disadvantage, discrimination and racism which are cited (CRE 1981) and as a consequence the stigmatisation of ethnic groups seems to give rise to forms of resistance and micro-strategies. The groups concerned felt that they were being treated unfairly, and the riots translated an aspiration for a more just society. The police and their treatment of young ethnic minority people caused tensions and enhanced hostility as documented in a high-profile public enquiry (Scarman 1981). They were the symbol of Babylon, a society perceived as stigmatising and repressive. The theme of economic, social and political exclusion of young ethnic minority people and their marginalisation was much quoted. From this vantage point the ideology of competitiveness against that of solidarity, individualism, the logic of the winner takes all, militated against social integration (Body-Gendrot 1995). It seemed logical that the only way to be taken into account was by protesting through violence. Relative frustration was posited as the result of thwarted expectations and comparisons with reference groups: poverty contrasted with the opulence of shop windows (Willems 1995).

Social disintegration is seen to derive from the erosion of institutions which traditionally played an integrating role such as schools, churches, working class neighbourhoods and communities, the welfare state (Joly 1996). Within such a context, the lack of meaning, hope and collective projects ran the risk of producing a demoralised, embittered population who had no stake in society. In these circumstances the 'social contract' was threatened (Rex 1996).

Continuities in a Changing Context

During the 1980s and 1990s there was a growth in the number of influences on debates on ethnic relations. The subject of 'ethnic' or 'race relations' or the study of racism has become a recognised area throughout the social sciences, broadening out from sociology to anthropology, cultural studies, geography and political science. This has been accompanied by the establishment of several competing theoretical explanations of the concepts involved. Alongside Rex's neo-Weberian approach, which has developed further within the European context, there are neo-Marxist, cultural studies, feminist-influenced theories, and post-colonial accounts. For the sake of coherence we will attempt to deal with these approaches separately but it should be understood that there is much overlapping and most writing does not fit neatly into any one category.

There has also been increased interest in the European dimension of the subject encouraged by greater opportunities for academic exchange and the development of the European Union. The incorporation of this perspective which involves formulating a response to the growth of racism and the harmonisation of immigration legislation has changed the way in which ethnic relations are theorised and researched in a number of ways which have combined with the theoretical and disciplinary influences on the subject.

Challenges to the Black/white dichotomy were taken further by researchers who called into question the unitary category of the 'ethnic minority community' which was highlighted when deep differences were revealed by the Rushdie affair (Asad 1990; Sahgal and Yuval-Davis 1992).

Recent debates about ethnic relations in Britain have focused on five main themes. Firstly, research has continued on old and new forms of discrimination and disadvantage. Secondly, problems have been identified with the use of the terms 'race' or 'racism' to analyse social relations, Thirdly, researchers have explored ways of understanding questions of racial, ethnic, religious and national identity in the context of changing social and political relations in contemporary societies. Fourthly, asylum and refugees within a European context have been examined. Finally, the limits and possibilities of citizenship in a multicultural society are being analysed.

Changing Modes of Discrimination and Disadvantage

Work has continued to analyse the changing modes of discrimination and disadvantage and reliable data has been produced through surveys. The most important source of data now comes from the ethnic group question in the Census of Population (although its categories are contestable and contested), and provides detailed information about population settlement, housing and households, employment and education (Owen 1994; Coleman and Salt, 1996; Peach 1996; Ratcliffe 1996; Karn 1997). The Labour Force Survey is another source which is useful for comparative purposes on levels and type of employment. Independent empirical work continued in the Policy Studies Institute's Third and Fourth National Surveys of Ethnic Minorities (Brown 1984, 1986; Modood 1997a and b; PSI 1991; Smith 1981).

When the CRE was set up in 1976, there was a need to establish a corpus of knowledge about indirect and institutional discrimination and to test the new powers of the law. A body of research was built up which linked to legal investigations and tribunal cases which showed in detail the way in which indirect discrimination operated in a variety of different contexts, in jobs such as nursing, teaching, accountancy, for doctors and in the armed forces (CRE 1988). Housing was another important area in which statistical data was used to show the systematic nature of discrimination in public sector provision and in the workings of estate agents (CRE 1984b and c). More recently work has been carried out to show systematic discrimination against the Irish in Britain (CRE 1997; Lloyd 1995) and to highlight the position of children. The CRE's formal powers of investigation were limited by a court case after its research into immigration control procedures so that it is not able to intervene in this area (CRE 1984a).

This has left researchers working closely with NGOs (particularly the Institute of Race Relations, the Runnymede Trust and Liberty) to focus on immigration policy. Studies have attempted to document trends in immigration law and to draw attention to new practices and injustices linked to the harmonisation of European migration laws (Fekete and Webber 1994; Gordon 1985). Danièle Joly has brought together much of this data in a theory of the new asylum regime in Europe (1996).

This growing body of evidence about different forms of discrimination is complemented by research on policies which aim to counter the effects of racism. Researchers have attempted to evaluate a variety of different municipal policy initiatives (Anthias and Yuval-Davis 1992; Gilroy 1986; Jenkins and Solomos 1987). This has involved the refinement of conceptual tools and a further understanding of the political context in which multiculturalism has taken place. There is surprisingly little work on anti-racism as a political movement, although recent comparative work by Lloyd (1996; Anthias and Lloyd in press) has attempted to escape from the formulation of anti-racism as the mirror image of racism and to theorise this within a social movement framework (see also Bonnett 1993; Stedward 1997).

For John Rex, the central theoretical question about multiculturalism is how respect for other cultures could be reconciled with equality. This work entered into a dialogue with other European formulations of the problem of difference/equality and involved a clarification of the meaning of ethnicity and ethnic minority cultures within a wide collaborative survey of European cities (Rex 1996, p. 4; 1996a; 1997). It also led to a discussion of the interactions between ethnicity and the nation state in the context of contemporary develop-ments and the formulation of the idea that the structural relationship between societies and the policies they develop could determine the mobilisation of transnational migrant communities which both contained the possibility of different forms of inter-group hostility and conflict (Rex 1997, p. 28).

'Race' and Racism

A critique which focused on the key concepts deployed within the sociology of race relations was launched from a neo-Marxist perspective by Robert Miles, who (influenced by the work of Colette Guillaumin) emphasised that the object of analysis should not be 'race' but racism (Miles 1989; 1993). He stressed that 'races' were a political construct within specific contexts of political and social regulation, and located the study of racism within the Marxist theory of social conflict. Building on earlier UNESCO work, Miles argued for the centrality of the concept of *racialisation* to refer to instances where 'social relations ... have been structured by the signification of human biological characteristics in such a way as to define and construct differentiated social collectivities' (Miles 1989, p. 75). He studied the nature of political action by migrant labour, which he argued took place through the modality of resistance to racism rather than through ethnic identity.

Miles has revised his earlier argument that colonialism was a central determinant of all racist ideologies and now proposes that theories of racism should also take into account 'precapitalist social relations within and beyond Europe'. This, he suggests, may yield implications for the formulation of policy and for antiracist struggle by giving us more information about whether racism has a universal character or whether it is specific to capitalism (Miles 1993, pp. 7–9). A historical analysis of migration in terms of class and nation formation, would allow for a wider understanding of who might be the 'victims' of racism and further distance the British debate from the Black/white dichotomy. This work has broader implications about the causes of migration and its links to uneven economic and democratic development throughout the world (Miles and Thranhardt 1995). Considerations on the status of New Right ideas has also given rise to work on the relationship between racism and nationalism (Miles 1993; Smith 1994). Further inquiries in a neo-Marxist mould have taken place over the relationship between the categories 'race' and class, particularly over the idea that there are a range of sites for social antagonism and resistance in contemporary Britain which go beyond a conventional class analysis (Hall and Jacques 1989; Sivanandan 1990). This discussion has given rise to further conceptualisation by Stuart Hall of 'new ethnicities'.

Ethnicity and Identity

The themes of ethnicity and ethnic groups are a constant subject of debate throughout the 1980s and into the 1990s. From its inception, it has been strongly influenced by American schools of thought. Assumptions on the primordial character of ethnicity were challenged under the influence of Barth's situational analysis (1969) pointing ethnicity and ethnic boundaries as socially constructed (Yinger 1986; Wallman 1986). On the other hand, the discussion on ethnicity also incorporated the dichotomy between self-definition (the in-group) and categorisation (ascription i.e. definitions imposed by the out-group), which take on board asymmetrical power relations and their inter-relationship (Jenkins 1997). Ethnicity has been portrayed as a resource (Khan 1997; Wallman 1986) but was generally not conceptualised as enclosure or withdrawal. However, an exclusive emphasis on ethnicity as a resource was sometimes criticised for indirectly 'blaming the victim' (Jenkins 1997).

Other scholars focused on the modes of social organisation of ethnic groups and in particular their associations (Rex, Joly and Wilpert 1987). Ethnic mobilisation developed as a key concept in the late 1980s and early 1990s (Rex and Drury 1994). It is argued in the 1990s that ethnicity and ethnic communities do not represent an attachment to traditions in opposition to modernity but are the means by which groups negotiate integration within the society of reception (Joly 1995): ethnicity is thus analysed as a basis for collective action. Islam and Muslim populations became a theme of particular salience as specific markers within the sociology of ethnic identity. A body of research has developed which turns its attention to Islam as a modern mobilising tool and studies the strategies of Muslim organisations within British society (Joly 1995; Nielsen 1999). Others focus on Islam as a process of identity construction (Modood and Werbner 1997).

In the nineties, the study of ethnicity was pursued through a criticism of its reification and through discussions on hybrid and shifting or diasporic identities (Hall 1990, Brah 1991), within the framework of the prominence of identity superseding that of class (Solomos and Back 1996). Recent studies of ethnicity stress the reversal of the victim's stigma through the culture of resistance and reconstruction of their history (Gilroy 1994; Joly 1998). Work influenced by post-structuralism and cultural studies showed a greater concern with cultural production and the politics of identity. The Cultural Studies critique of the sociology of 'race', analysed the processes by which 'race' was constructed as a contested social and political relation within contemporary modernity. Stuart Hall argued that the debate about 'race' had shifted from an initial use of the term 'Black' within struggles over their access to the rights of representation and the contestation of their marginality. According to Hall, by the late 1980s the struggle had become more one of a 'politics of representation' (Hall 1992; Hall and du Gay 1996). The insights provided by Hall's work involves 'a recognition that the central issues of race always appear historically in articulation, in a formation with other categories and divisions and are constantly crossed and re-crossed by the categories of class, gender and ethnicity' (Hall and du Gay 1996, p. 444).

The notion that collective identities could be powerful ways of coordinating action and creating solidarity, led to work which focused on the development of a multiplicity of political identities (Gilroy 1987). Gilroy suggests that such identities are social movements which are separate from class relations. His work on the 'Black Atlantic world' develops Clifford's work on 'travelling cultures' to explore relationships between 'race', ethnicity, culture and nationality from the standpoint of Black British citizens, challenging Black ethnic absolutism (Clifford 1992; Gilroy 1993a and b). Another approach has been to develop the idea of diaspora as 'an interpretive frame for analysing the economic, political and cultural modalities of historically specific forms of migrancy' (Brah 1996, p. 16; Cohen 1996; Anthias 1998). Researchers in the field of cultural studies have investigated the role of literature, popular media and other cultural forms in changing forms of ethnicity and 'race' within studies of the dialogue between Black and white working-class cultures or the construction of 'race' in literature and the cinema (Cohen 1992; Dyer 1988).

Empirical work on the political mobilisation of Asians in Birmingham has illustrated how these racialised constructions operate and examined the relations between Black and white youth in inner city areas; popular cultures of racism (especially in football) have drawn attention to the conditions in which some racisms are muted and other forms seem to flourish (Back 1995; Solomos and Back 1996). Spurred by Stuart Hall's challenge to white English people to understand who they are in order to surmount the post-imperial crisis of identity and to focus onto the perpetrators of racism, there have been several analyses of the impact of different racisms on the white population, and attempts to develop understandings of 'whiteness' and 'being normal' (Dyer 1988; Hall (1989), *After Dread and Anger*, BBC Radio 4, cited in Solomos and Back 1996, p. 25). This links with Miles's interest in the idea of a European racism.

Theoretical work derived from feminism has also developed since the 1980s, strongly influenced by work from the USA and more recently Australia and Europe. Research has gradually been moving away from a compartment-alised view of 'race', class and gender, to view the relationship between each form of structuring. Feminist writers of ethnic minority origins have intervened in debates about the sociopolitical context of contemporary racism (Carby 1982). There is debate about the limits of the usefulness of western feminism in relation to the question of 'race' and the relationship between racism and sexism and on links between racism and gender inequality (Anthias and Yuval-Davis 1992; James and Busia 1993). Research has covered the role of women in the migration process, family relations, the employment and social position of migrant women (Anthias 1998). One very specific aspect of this work is the analysis of the growth of illegal highly exploited employment and of the 'grey' economy which has had a significant impact on some women in ethnic minority communities (Phizacklea 1995; Westwood and Bachu 1988).

Researchers are increasingly aware of the global or transnational aspects of ethnic relations conceived in terms of theories of diaspora or of cultural fusion (Back 1993; Brah 1996; Gilroy 1993; Hall 1996, Pries 1999). As we have seen with research concerned about the new regime in immigration law, there is also a growing concern about the new Europe which can be associated with earlier critiques of Eurocentrism.

Post-colonial theory is a body of interdisciplinary writings which attempts to bring together many of these trends while respecting the new respect for context. This combines anti-colonial cultural practices with the idea of transcending or superseding the parameters of colonialism which may also include the idea of neo-colonialism and post-colonial migration (Childs and Williams 1997, pp. 3–6). Influenced by the work of writers such as Homi Bhabha (1994), Franz Fanon (1975), Edward Said (1985; 1993) and Gayatri Spivak (1990), the post-colonial approach emphasises historical research on the changing use of racial symbols and accounts of the experiences of colonialism. It proposes a critique of the continuing discourse of colonialism within, for example, the idea of globalisation, and questions the hegemony of the West and of modernity. This approach has, *inter alia*, highlighted the processes of racial and gender identifications experienced by the colonised during the colonial and post-colonial periods (Bhabha 1994; Ware 1992; Williams and Chrisman 1993; Young 1995). It proposes a reversal of the victims' stigma through an emphasis on resistance, and the reconstruction of their history (Gilroy 1993b).

Whereas these theories have been developed by those pursuing cultural studies rather than a sociological approach and within the concept of diasporic culture, John Rex has made a separate contribution to the study of colonial and post-colonial society and post-colonial migration to the metropolis. Thus, in the later edition of his book *Race Relations in Sociological Theory*, he argues with M.G. Smith about the nature of plural societies and develops his own account of the economic and political aspects of colonial stratification and of the changes which come about through the achievement of political independence. This involves some consideration of the relation between Marxist and Fanonist theories of revolution. This analysis is then extended to deal with post-colonial migrants to imperial metropolises.

Asylum and Refugees

Research on asylum and refugees has so far developed as a discrete area of investigation and remained for a long time on the margins of hot debates in the field of ethnic and race relations, except among lawyers (Goodwin-Gill 1983). This is in stark contrast to political and social domains where asylum policies occupied a prominent place on governments' agenda, and with substantial growth in the numbers of asylum seekers and refugees. Until the mid-1980s these were only narrow policy-related pieces of research mostly carried out by NGOs (Joly and Cohen 1989). Research on a European harmonisation process was pioneered by Joly (Joly et al. 1992; Joly 1996). This area is currently generating more interest among social scientists: on asylum policies, settlement policies (Jones 1982; Carey-Wood 1997), and refugee groups' strategies (Kay and Miles 1992). Joly (1999) is currently developing the framework of a new asylum regime in Europe paired with a theoretical tool for the analysis of refugee types. This area of research is generating increasing interest among geographers, sociologists, psychologists and social scientists.

Citizenship

Finally, the theme of citizenship is being revisited and updated in the context of European unification and tensions within nation-states (Dummett and Nicol 1990; Juss 1993; Plant 1988; Bottomore 1992; Layton-Henry 1990). New categories of citizenship are posited facilitating dual belonging (Smith 1999).

Conclusion

During the 1980s the British government had taken the lead in Europe in implementing neoliberal economic policies. A strategy of privatisation of public utilities bought the market principle into the remaining areas of a reduced public service sector. This, coupled with the restructuring of industry, has given rise to higher levels of precarious, part-time or temporary employment or long-term structural unemployment (Hutton 1996).

The analysis of the authoritarian state current in the late 1970s (CCCS 1982) proved inadequate to encompass the radical nature of the changes which have since taken place in the political context of ethnic relations. Theoretical debates have moved towards an agreement about the existence of a multiplicity or spectrum of racisms but also the fragmentation of the idea of 'Black' in favour of ideas about cultural differentiation which are producing cultural syncretisms. There is also a consensus about the need for the political agendas involved in conceptualising racism to be made explicit so that they are not separated from the historical and political context and within processes of social regulation and the formation of identity. Racism is increasingly analysed through its relations with other social relations around gender, sexuality, culture and institutional politics.

The past two decades have not been propitious for the influence of research in ethnic relations. Under Thatcherism in the 1980s, the government was driven by its own ideological imperatives, and any change of direction was interpreted as a defeat or a 'U-turn'. The success of government was supposed to be shown in its inflexibility of purpose rather than in its responsiveness to public opinion. However, some research reports did have an incontrovertible impact, even though their findings were only adopted on a selective basis.

The most notable examples are the Scarman (1981), Swann (1985) and the Burnage reports (Macdonald 1989). Other research, such as that concerning young Black people and the police or racist violence, has had a less direct impact but tends to 'burrow a way' and is developing an incremental impact.

The election of the 'New' Labour government in May 1997 has introduced a rather more complex (and mixed) situation. The European context continues to be highly significant especially for immigration policy and the research agenda follows this closely (Koffman 1998). However, the government did make some initial concessions, notably to the primary purpose rule which had overshadowed many attempts at family reunification. New Deal policies to alleviate unemployment have been criticised for failing to tackle racism in job placements (Lock 1998) and education policies have failed to address racism in exclusion from school (CARF 1998). In a climate where racist violence continues to blight people's lives, the government was acclaimed for setting up a public inquiry into the death of Stephen Lawrence (in April 1993) and produced a comprehensive report into the surrounding events (Macpherson 1999). While the operational impact of the report on policing remains to be evaluated, the refined definition of institutional racism is significant (para 6.34). It suggests a future research agenda on difficult questions such as the historical and social phenomena shaping social relations and the limitations of social reform in a context of racism (Solomos 1999). These new developments demand a more holistic research approach which seeks to establish an independent political perspective on the problem of racism, particularly in institutional contexts. This will be enhanced by the

World Conference on Racism (2001) preceded by a Council of Europe conference (2000).

The priority accorded asylum in the Treaty of Amsterdam has generated the expansion of research programmes on this theme sponsored by the European Commission. This is paralleled in the UK by the introduction of a new Immigration and Asylum Act (1999); the Home Office is launching two research programmes respectively on asylum policies in Europe and on asylum-seekers' reception in the UK. The Rowntree Foundation has commissioned a report on the reception and settlement of refugees and asylum-seekers with a view to ascertain research needs. Thus this area of research is likely to expand.

The underlying logic informing government policy remains that of the market and policies are framed within the twin static concepts of social exclusion and globalisation, which emphasise the impossibility of social and political intervention and focus instead on individual responsibility (Levitas 1996).

Chapter Two

Ethnicity and Labour Migrants' Mode of Settlement

Introduction

The main protagonists in our study are the children, possibly the grandchildren of labour migrants who came from the Caribbean to the UK after World War Two. The focus of study is the consequences of migration involving the interaction between those groups and the majority society, in their process of settlement. In the UK they are commonly designated as ethnic minority groups. Where young people are concerned who were born and brought up in the reception country of their parents, an additional set of questions is raised which have their own specificity. This chapter examines a few dimensions of ethnicity and the formation of ethnic groups; this includes debates about the contemporariness of these concepts for young people of immigrant origin.

Despite the increasing salience of ethnic groups and ethnicity it is worth noting that these are not universally recognised as significant categories by majority societies and even by sociologists. France is a case in point where policy makers do not acknowledge ethnic minorities; this is matched by the researchers' focus on the political participation of these populations (Leveau and Kepel 1988), or their position as (immigrant) workers (de Rudder et al. 1994) rather than their ethnicity. In France, ethnicity, if it is contemplated as a possibility, tends to be conceived as a purely private business which might not even stand in the path of assimilation as Lapeyronnie (1993) argues; so much so that he sometimes uses the terms assimilation and integration interchangeably. The concepts of ethnies and ethnicity are often perceived to belong to anthropological studies of primitive societies and not to modern societies where reference to them is deemed as a derogatory connotation. Simon-Barouh (1982) sees in the term 'ethnic minorities' an indication of dependency and domination. Wieviorka (1994) equates the terms with notions of inferiorisation. This is not the case in the Anglo-Saxon world, where sociologists have frequently championed the concept and social reality of ethnicity and ethnic groups. How can these concepts help us to understand the modes of settlement of immigrants and their strategies?

Modes of Settlement

Three main processes can be observed in immigrants' modes of settlement. *Assimilation* refers to the complete integration of immigrants as individuals which does not leave a space for cultural or any other difference on a group basis. Until the 1950s, assimilation was often assumed to be the path which immigrants would follow under structural pressures to do so from the society of reception. In the USA the immigrants had gone with a project of settlement and were expected to become Americanised. In Europe assimilation was the expectation of the receiving society as illustrated by assimilationist measures (until the 1960s in the UK, for instance). Social scientists had similar view, such as Park who notes that labour was imported as a commodity, but what came were 'humans like ourselves' (1950, p. 150). What follows in his opinion is a cycle which is 'apparently progressive and irreversible,' taking the form of 'contacts, competition, accommodation and eventual assimilation' (p. 151). This view is shared by several other sociologists including Eisenstadt (1954) who analyses the stages traversed by the immigrant before the 'process of absorption' is completed. However, this is not solely the mark of a functionalist approach and it can also fit in a Marxist model. It is possible that the immigrants who came as workers will develop a class consciousness alongside autochthonous workers and participate in the conflicts of the reception society. Assimilation here means joining in the organisations of the latter, i.e. trade unions and political parties, and their struggles; in this instance the main bases for the immigrants' involvement in collective action are class issues. Immigrant workers in France in the first half of the twentieth century are often quoted to illustrate this process. Another possibility is that the immigrants and their offspring take part in action against discrimination and racism, to claim full participation in the host society on an equal footing (as in SOS Racisme and France Plus).

Separation is less common in European societies. Instances of separation of racial/ethnic/migrant groups are quoted within the framework of discussions on pluralism and the plural society. Furnivall's (1939) colonial society is the clearest example of separation as ethnic groups only met as individuals in the market place but had their separate cultures, institutions and economic niches. Glazer and Moynihan (1970), concerned at the level of racial violence in the southern states of the USA, warned that the alternatives had shifted away from an option between assimilation and ethnic group status; it 'now seems to lie somewhere between ethnic group status and separatism' (1970, p. xxiii). The level of separation/segregation enforced in colonial and post-colonial societies (such as South Africa) is not to be found in contemporary Western Europe, while ghettos in the classic sense of the word (as in the Warsaw Ghetto) no longer exist in modern Western societies. However, some degree of separation may occur, mostly as a result of discrimination and racism, and may lead to marginalisation.

Integration is taken to refer to varying degrees and levels of social relationships and participation in the majority society while securing the preservation of difference which leads to the formation of distinctive groups. Thus it does not include assimilation. However, this integration can take a variety of forms and paths and take place at different levels: social, economic and political. The groups which interest us particularly in this context are ethnic groups, to which we now turn.

Ethnicity and Ethnic Groups

Primordial and Situational Definitions

If we accept that ethnic groups can be found outside primitive societies, who can they refer to? What we are looking at are ethnic groups that may arise as a consequence of migration and are not territorially rooted and based. According to Yinger (1986, p. 23), the term 'ethnic group' has expanded its meaning to embrace a great diversity of categories, such as

> a sub-societal group that clearly shares a common descent and cultural background ..., persons sharing a former citizenship although diverse culturally ..., pan-cultural groups of persons of widely different cultural and societal backgrounds who, however, can be identified as 'similar' on the basis of language, race or religion, mixed with broadly similar statuses.

This definition undoubtedly enhances the relevance of the concept for the immigrant groups we are considering in Western Europe. A series of varying criteria are advanced by social scientists to define ethnic groups (Geertz 1963; Gordon 1978; Smith 1986; Yinger 1986; Rex 1995; Drury 1995, to cite only a few).

The paradigm has shifted from primordial assumptions of ethnicity to a situational interpretation. Primordialists like Geertz (1963) stressed the 'attachment' based on kinship, common residence, language, religion and custom. The 'warmth' of emotional links (affective ties) is emphasised together with the cultural content. For situationists the cultural 'content' plays little role since what is paramount is the socially constructed 'boundary', the distinction between 'us and them' (Barth 1969). One important consequence of this approach is that ethnicity and ethnic groups cannot exist on their own. They arise against or in contrast with others, other minority ethnic groups and/or the majority group in a 'system of ethnicities' (Yinger 1986). Moreover, for situationists, another important tenet of ethnicity is that it is situational and constitutes a 'resource' in the competition for resources (Saifullah Khan 1977; Wallman 1986); ethnicity is used and activated for economic/political or other ends, so that the markers called upon to establish the distinction between 'us and them' may change according to need (Wallman 1986). In Wallman's view although the markers most often used are territoriality, history, language, economic considerations and symbolic identifications, there is no logical limit to their numbers. None of these are intrinsically ethnic but can become 'converted into ethnicity' (Wallman 1986, p. 230). This implies a distinctly instrumental connotation.

Gemeinschaft or Gesellschaft?

The discussion above introduces an ambiguity as to what kind of groups are ethnic groups: the warmth of the relationship described by the primordialists implies a notion of community while the instrumentalism of the situationists implies associations for a purpose (within the arena of *Gesellschaft*). Wieviorka (1994) associates them with tradition (community) while Glazer and Moynihan (1975) equate them with interest groups. Rex (1986) even hesitates to call them groups at all, because he sees that the representative aspect might be lacking and he refers to them as quasi groups. However, if one examines the modes of social organisation of immigrants/ethnic minorities, one finds that this dichotomy between *Gesellschaft* (modern society with its associations) and *Gemeinschaft* (community) is difficult to sustain. In the case of ethnic minority groups, they are not necessarily exclusive of each other but rather complementary. Associations may precede community as in the case of Sparkbrook Pakistanis (Rex and Moore 1967) but they do not disappear when a community is established. On the contrary, the more complete the community, more numerous and thriving the associations (Joly 1995). The latter do not either serve purely instrumental purposes but also provide moral, social and emotional support (Joly 1995). The mobilisation of ethnic groups in conflict with the rest of society follows distinctly modern patterns with a purpose while their internal mode of social organisation and relations are those of community. Even organisations which existed in the society of origin, such as mosques, assume different additional characteristics in the society of reception, with regard to their methods, functions and role and their internal structures (Joly 1987). They act as interest groups in the society of reception but they are also characterised by warm and close social relations invested with emotional and moral significance.

Ethnic Mobilisation

However, the violent conflicts involving ethnic groups which one can sometimes witness lead us to consider more closely the question of ethnic mobilisation. In the first place it is necessary to distinguish between ethnicity and ethnic mobilisation. Although ethnic mobilisation is a frequent occurrence, does an ethnic group have to be 'mobilised' to constitute an ethnic group? Clearly the answer to this question rests on what is meant by 'mobilised'. If being conscious of oneself and conducting activities as a group means being mobilised, then ethnic mobilisation is concomitant with ethnicity. However, it is generally accepted that ethnic mobilisation goes beyond this level of action; it presupposes acting together in the competition for resources, political purposes and gains.

> Ethnic mobilisation can be defined as a process in which members of an ethnic group, in specific and relevant situations: first, develop heightened levels of group consciousness vis-à-vis other groups; second, employ cultural criteria or other symbols of their unity ... to sharpen the boundaries between themselves and others; third, prepare, organise and consolidate their resources in order to take action and fourth, take action, usually of a political kind, in order to defend, promote and/or create collective as opposed to individual goals. (Drury 1994, p. 15)

There are varying views as to what factors and circumstances lead to ethnic mobilisation. One widely accepted explanation for the mobilisation of ethnic groups is that they feel excluded from sharing equally opportunities and resources (Bonacich 1972 and Wieviorka 1994). Another position is that mobilisation by ethnic groups occurs when they have become socially and economically mobile because they feel the need to defend their gains against competitors, particularly during a recession (Olzac and Nagel 1986). These two explanations may seem contradictory but they can be analysed as complementary if they are understood within the framework of a class system wherein groups mobilise, to acquire access to resources and opportunities, which they do not have or to defend such access which they have to some extent acquired and which they fear losing. A third explanation, the resource mobilisation theory, focuses on levels of group cohesiveness and organisational strength (Jenkins 1983). Two major aspects of ethnic mobilisation are strengthened by the resource mobilisation theory; a good organisational base with leaders, associations, and organisational skills are conducive to more effective action while ethnic group consciousness is 'heightened' if there exist dense networks, associations and activities; but the multiplicity of leaders runs the risk of fragmenting the community.

Structure and Actors, Categorisation and Self-definition

A number of questions have to be discussed. Can an ethnic group exist as an objective reality or does it require consciousness of itself as a *sine qua non?* Is it comparable to a class in a partially objective manner, in the way that Marx (1973, pp. 238–9) analyses classes as determined by their relations to the means of production:

> The small peasant proprietors form an immense mass, the members of which live in the same situation but do not enter into manifold relationships with each other. Their mode of operation isolates them instead of bringing them into mutual intercourse. This isolation is strengthened by the wretched state of France's means of communication and by the poverty of the peasants. Their place of operation, the smallholding, permits no division of labour in its cultivation, no application of science and therefore no diversity of development, variety of talent, or wealth of social relationships. Each individual peasant family is almost self-sufficient; it directly produces the greater part of its own consumption and therefore obtains its means of life more through exchange with nature than through intercourse with society. The smallholding, the peasant, and the family; next door, another smallholding, another peasant, and another family. A bunch of these makes up a village, and a bunch of villages makes up a department. Thus the great mass of the French nation is formed by the simple addition of isomorphous magnitudes, much as potatoes in a sack form a sack of potatoes. In so far as millions of families live under economic conditions of existence that separate their mode of life, their interests and their cultural formation from those of the other classes and bring them into conflict with those classes, they form a class.

Despite the seemingly 'objective' character of the primordialist interpretation of ethnicity (i.e. what 'givens' the members of the group are born into), both primordialists and situationists appear to share the view that the actors concerned have to be aware of themselves as an ethnic group, either in the form of 'emotional attachment' or 'resource mobilisation'. One the main criteria often quoted in the definition of an ethnic group is also that its members must be involved in collective activity: according to Yinger (1986, p. 22):

> An ethnie exists in the full sense when three conditions are present: a segment of a larger society is seen by others to be different in some combination of the following characteristics – language, religion, race and ancestral homeland with its related culture; the members also perceive themselves in that way; and they participate in shared activities built around their (real or mythical) common origin and culture.

These two prerequisites, consciousness of self and collective activity, give a central role to the social actors involved (Jenkins 1986, p. 176). However, one issue remains unclear. Are those 'shared activities' actually carried out collectively, with the consciousness of acting in the name of the group and as a group, or do they include any practices, including individual practices partaking of specific cultural codes?

On the other hand, the situational approach gives scope for an enhanced influence of structural factors in the formation of ethnic groups. Could this make them a function of the structural set-up of the reception society, i.e. whether or not the institutions of the latter provide a space for recognition, negotiation and potential gains which would generate a basis for group formation? In this sense can the Anglo-Saxon world be said to 'create' ethnic groups through the potential advantages awarded to them and the seeking out of community 'representatives'? In societies where there is no official nor public recognition of ethnic groups as in France, for example, political mobilisation as an ethnic group does not yield obvious benefits. In such society ethnic groups, if there were such, traditionally confined their ethnicity to the private domain. This, however, did not preclude a dense network of community associations and activities as a group in the private arenas of life (Hily and Poinard 1987: Campani et al. 1987).

Most definitions of the ethnic group comprise perception from outside and from inside. The former is generally referred to as 'categorisation' (Jenkins 1997). One must ask what happens when the categorisation from outside does not match the perception from inside. This is bound up with the power relations which the class system entails as the ethnic groups we are concerned with are placed in a situation of exploitation and subordination in the lower echelons of the class structure. It is difficult to claim rather mechanically that the structural situation of people and groups automatically leads to consciousness.

But the mobilisation of ethnic groups is related also to the structural disadvantage in which they are placed and the discriminatory ideology and practices concomitant with it. It is thus possible that the discrimination accompanying ascription from outside or categorisation by the dominant group might lead to new forms of solidarity and consciousness as a group; it is not inconceivable but also not inevitable that the latter might then develop and mobilise as an ethnic group.

Private and Public Ethnicity

One must be careful not to confuse ethnicity and ethnic mobilisation. Indeed, according to Barth himself, ethnicity constitutes a resource in a way of differentiating oneself from others but not necessarily for engagement in political action (Barth 1969). One needs to introduce the notion of private and public into this debate. Ethnicity may remain private while ethnic mobilisation itself is necessarily a public manifestation of ethnicity. The mobilisation of these populations does not have to assume an ethnic character but may lead to ethnic mobilisation when the ascription from outside and other structural factors (discrimination, rejection, resource allocation) prompts a group to turn some of its characteristics into ethnic markers. However, this is not inevitable. For instance in the UK and the USA it appears that the institutional legitimation of ethnicity concomitant with concrete advantages attached to it has led to private ethnicities becoming public and even to the creation of 'imagined' ethnicities engaged in ethnic mobilisation. In France, on the other hand, while discrimination and racism may sometimes entail the affirmation of ethnico-religious identity, it usually generates action on another basis as anti-racists or 'immigrants' (de Rudder et al. 1994). The long absent and then limited legitimation of ethnic associations caused these to become an instrumental tool for the purposes of individual advancement and not group projects (Withol de Wenden 1994), while the groups who were not discriminated against restricted their ethnicity to the private sphere (Lapeyronnie 1993). The strategies adopted by immigrants are strongly influenced by the agenda of action and the political culture written in the reception society, and secondarily in the society of origin. In societies where ethnicity and ethnic minorities find a channel pre-existing in the structure of that society, they will be more likely to develop and become public. In societies where historically these channels were not open and where the logic of action was more solely one of class, ethnicity is less prominent. When the minority populations concerned were themselves raised in former colonial societies which inherited the same mode of functioning, they may have acquired these even prior to migration. These migrant workers are at the same time members of the working class and potential members of an ethnic group. They may orientate their group identification and collective action as members of the working class (as in the French model), as members of an ethnic minority group (the American model), or as both (often the British model). In most situations both identifications coexist and either of them may become more or less salient according to the circumstances but one generally takes precedence on a more stable basis for group formation, forms of actions and mobilisation. Currently ethnic groups and ethnic mobilisation are acquiring greater salience as the crisis of Western European societies jeopardises their habitual modes of functioning with the demise of both universalist national and social grand projects (Wieviorka 1994).

The Relationship with Integration

The question is often posed rather simplistically as to whether ethnic groups help or hamper the integration of their members into majority society. It would be more appropriate to ask about the dialectical relationship between integration and the formation of ethnic groups as these interact dynamically. Indeed, the opportunities or incentives for integration and the forms of integration available will have an impact not only on the salience of ethnicity and the formation of an ethnic group but also on its role in the integration process. Lapeyronnie (1993, p. 30) sees ethnicity as an intrinsic part of the integration process: 'l'affirmation d'une identité italienne particulière est construite dans le rapport entretenu avec le pays d'accueil' (the affirmation of a specific Italian identity is constructed through the relationship with the reception country – my translation). It is also conceivable that segregation and discrimination measures lead to enclosure of the ethnic group (de Rudder et al. 1994). This may bring about an affirmation of specificity in order to assert a space of dignity (Lapeyronnie 1993). More often some form of ethnic mobilisation will arise not only to protect the group but also to gain opportunities and resources in the majority society. In terms of the modes of settlement of ethnic minorities, it is clear that the ethnic group when it occurs generally contributes both to a greater interaction with the reception society and a preservation of itself as a community/ies. It entertains a project of self perpetuation but usually not as a segregated entity on the margins of society; on the contrary, it is fighting for a place in the society of settlement complete with rights on a par with autochthones and the right to preserve its difference: these are the dual objectives in its collective action. It has become a prevalent view that the ethnic group helps integration rather than hampers it (Ballis Lal 1986). Wirth (1928) had argued long ago that it provides a secure environment from which to venture into the big wide world of the reception society. On the other hand, ethnic groups may even be deliberately used by the governing bodies as a means of control (Schierup 1994). At any rate in almost all cases ethnic mobilisation is a positive declaration of engagement with the reception society; this is true even in the case of violent confrontation.

Ethnicisation and the Deconstruction of Ethnicities

The debate on ethnicity and ethnic group has thrown up new questions. In the nineties the field of ethnic and migration research has been characterised by two distinct trends which translate parallel phenomena in contemporary societies. On the one hand an emphasis was placed on a re-ethnification or re-ethnicisation of society (Friedman 1997), and on the other hand this view was criticised or complemented from a variety of vantage points. New concepts have also been developed to account for processes taking place among migrant groups, such as hybridity and transnational communities.

Ethnification

It is posited that nation states are undergoing a process of ethnification which includes indigenisation, regionalisation, localisation of identification, and both the ethnification of migrants and nationals (Friedman 1997). This is deemed to be expressed through a return to roots and to fixed identifications. Indigenous peoples throughout the world are stating new claims to territory and culture conveyed via nationally and internationally based organisations. It is also reflected through UN declarations and an increased recognition by states. With regard to migrants, one increasingly notices the apparent formation of ethnic groups/ethnic communities in the country of reception. Ethnic groups and ethnic processes of group identification are seen to have occupied the space left by the disintegration of national institutions and class-based forms of organisation (Wieviorka 1992). It is argued that this process is augmented by universal deregulation and the unqualified priority awarded to market competition (Z. Bauman 1997).

It is even posited that images of ethnic communities such as *Gemeinschaft* underpin research designs on immigrants revealing an ethnicised theoretical bias (Caglar 1997). Ethnicity has also been increasingly portrayed as a resource whilst an exclusive emphasis on ethnicity in this manner was sometimes criticised for indirectly 'blaming the victim' (Jenkins 1997). In a process of ethnic mobilisation, minority groups are shown to negotiate with the majority society to put forward their interests through their associations (Candappa and Joly 1994; Rex and Drury 1995). Abundant research on ethnic groups provides evidence of their mode of social organisation (Rex, Joly and Wilpert 1987). Moreover, from the mid-1970s to today, what is noticeable is a growing ethnification of public social arenas, and identity politics (Friedman 1997; Joly 1995). This enhances the propensity among community leaders to represent culture as a monolithic body of lifestyles and convictions which the whole group shares in (G. Bauman 1997) and which enables them to state claims to recognition and rights. However, this may pose a problem to those who might not choose to identify themselves in this way such as people from those communities born in countries of reception who wish to be able to partake of both heritages. In much of Europe and certainly in all the Anglo-Saxon world, multiculturalist policies have entailed an institutionalisation of culture and ethnicity in the public space; but this also implies that only those specific groups and identities will be publicly acknowledged and granted rights/ advantages (Caglar 1997). In a more universalist light, some social scientists have interpreted the increasing salience of ethnicity as a broadening of democratic rights: cultural rights are advanced as pertaining to the realm of democratic rights with a 'cultural democracy' elaborating on political and social democracy (Touraine 1997).

The dominant discourse is said to ethnicise further more groups of immigrant origin. Through equating culture, community and ethnic identity; as a consequence, ethnicity runs the risk of becoming 'naturalised' (G. Bauman 1997). Within majority society this means that racists may use differences as bases for irreconcilable and or threatening cultural distinctiveness: they soon reach the conclusion that those groups must be kept at a distance, segregated or expelled (Wieviorka 1997). Extreme right organisations tend to emphasise difference to stress pure national identity and culture in order to reinforce the in-group.

In countries where the dominant discourse and the official position of the state continue to deny the acceptability of diverse ethnic identities within the national polity and the city, this has been challenged by a position defending their entitlement to recognition within the scope of difference and equality (Touraine 1997). However, in societies where multicultural policies have been implemented, the 'essentialism' attributed to the notion of ethnic groups and ethnicity has been questioned. Is there space for a middle way?

Hybridisation and Creolisation

One important school of thought has seized upon what they consider an essentialist tendency in research focusing on ethnic groups and ethnicity as objects. The study of ethnicity is then pursued through a criticism of its reification and through discussions on hybrid, shifting or diasporic identities (Hall 1990; Brar 1991). In a critique of the notion of cultures as homogeneous, bounded, reified wholes, a number of concepts are advanced such as hyphenated, hybrid and creolised identities. The complexities of synchretic cultures among youth of immigrant origin is also explained as liminality and rhizomes, in terms of the transformation of symbols, identities or public roles (Back 1996). All refer to the mixture of cultures particularly as applied to people of immigrant origin, born and brought up in their parents' country of reception. The bell is said to toll for the innocent essential Black subject, to be replaced by a positive conception of the ethnicity of the margin, and a cultural diaspora-isation through a process of hybridisation, 'cut-and-mix' (Hall 1992). These concepts are often perceived as a challenge to the nation-state (Friedman 1997). They are supposed to destabilise or subvert hierarchies imposed on differences (Caglar 1997). The enemy is what is 'bounded' and thus essentialist (Friedman 1997). Hybridisation dons a normative dimension and is construed as a politically correct solution.

However, a number of questions must be addressed to the advocates of hybridisation and anti-essentialism. Are all notions of ethnic groups and ethnicity condemned to essentialism? Would this entail the evacuation of ethnicity and ethnic group as analytical categories? What of ethnicity as a situationalist resource in the Barthian model? Barth deconstructed culture through his 'situational' analysis of ethnicity, which he divested of its essentialism (Barth 1969). Is there not an incompatibility between the supposed essentialism of ethnicity and its often exercised instrumental use? How can ethnicity as a basis for collective action be analysed within the framework of hybridisation? How do these hybrid cultures relate to forms of organisation and action which develop in the course of political action (Rex 1997)? Even the political correctness of hybridisation and related concepts founder on the mobilisation of ethnicity and ethnic groups for the purpose of political action. Moreover, it is also doubtful whether hybridisation and creolisation adequately challenge essentialism: it has been pointed out that the notion of mixture assumes the prior existence of bounded pure 'essentialist' cultures (J. Friedman 1997).

A more serious interrogation bears on the capacity of creolisation to defy hierarchies and oppression; in some cases it might represent the opposite as in Central America where the mestizo concept was used as a tool of colonialism, the 'hybrids' being associated with the elite ruling over the Indians (J. Friedman 1997). Finally, the celebration of cultural diversity and hybridity often overlooks discrimination and exclusion based both on ethnicity and class; it fails to effectively challenge the discrimination which ethnic groups suffer. It has been argued that hybrid identities are generally the attributes of a particular class, the intelligentsia 'who can afford a cosmopolitan identity' (J. Friedman 1997). One could add that the intellectuals who advocate such concepts seem to propose not an analysis of society but a subjective description of their own situation posited as an analytical category for other groups in society. Such an approach more or less corresponds to Honoré de Balzac's word about the novel, a 'mirror' passing along the way; it focuses on a mere reflection of social reality and does not go beyond apparent fragmentation and disintegration. Sociologists in this field would do better to dig below the surface, the underpinning structures and social interactions which give rise to particular formulations of ethnicities or other forms of group identifications.

Within the modern framework of the nation state, hybridity has been advanced as a challenge to the dominant norm which imposes fixed categories. It is a fact that 'hybrids' within the British colonial regime (in India, for example) were often perceived as a threat to the established order and its ideology of racial superiority: offspring of mixed parentage were thus considered a subversive element. However, the same school of thought which posits hybridity as a counter-norm also suggests that it is becoming the prevailing characteristic of contemporary society as enhanced through globalisation. In this case, can hybridity keep its pertinence as a norm and counter-norm at the same time? It is counterposed to the essentialism of ethnic categories which is deemed to be conservative and conformist. However, social reality is more complex: what can be observed is a two-pronged process. The demise of the nation state and its homogenous assimilationist model (as in France) may lead to an ethnicisation with some dimension of resistance and subversion through the mobilisation of ethnic groups who challenge the dominant norm. On the other hand, another process may take place through which youths question both the monolithic model of the nation-state and that of the ethnic group. They adopt a critical distance vis-à-vis both, and rely on one code to criticise the other, respectively. One is no longer faced with a binary opposition along the lines of assimilation-resistance, but what is happening is that young people may make use of a variety of registers. This capacity to manipulate a plurality of codes and to adopt a critical attitude vis-à-vis different registers seems to match mechanisms evidenced by current theories on socialisation.

Those theories challenge functionalist approaches on actors' integrated models and stress the plurality of the subject as well as the increasing importance of their capacity to reflect on and criticise social norms (Verhoeven 1997, pp. 209–22). What needs to be asked is whether the social individual is capable of such analytical reflection and can muster the use of several registers. To what extent does this happen and does it constitute a significant trend? Does there still exist a collective mobilisation among those groups and on what basis?

Transnational Communities

Another school of social scientists broaches the issue from the vantage point of international migration. These theories take on board the role of the social actors involved, i.e. the migrants. Theories on the individual motivations of migration do not help much to analyse its social effects. One can gain a better insight through what Massey et al. (1993) point out as the collective decision-making unit and its objective but also the distinction which they establish between what causes the initiation of migration and what causes its perpetuation. This analysis shows that migration decisions are made by larger units than the individual, such as households or extended families with a view not solely to maximising total income but also to diversifying sources of income as an insurance against a variety of risks. Migration is thereafter perpetuated as migrants create transnational networks which constitute social capital. These theories will also have wide-ranging implications for the analysis of effects of migration on both sending and receiving countries.

Another explanation pertains to notions of relative deprivation whereby status and income improvements in the country of origin are sought relative to other families involved in migration. This logic is sustainable only if links are maintained between the migrants, former migrants and non-migrants in origin and destination areas. Network theory analysing ties of kinship, friendship and shared community of origin is thereafter used to account for the perpetuation of migration as a self-sustaining diffusion process (Massey et al. 1993). It has been stated that contemporary international migration is no longer simply the case of a place of origin and a place of arrival as was traditionally assumed (Pries 1999). What is becoming apparent is that this migration is not irrevocable and that links with the sending countries are not severed even after a long period of settlement (Faist 1999). New theories of migration propose that migration flows assume a new and unique quality while new transnational realities are developing in and through international migration networks.

As a consequence it is argued that qualitatively new social groups are being established in new social fields in the shape of deterritorialised social spaces (Pries 1999). To explain the factors for the creation and maintenance of transnational social spaces, theories of social capital (Bourdieu, quoted by Pries 1999) and cumulative causation are called upon. Migrants' networks are identified as a form of social capital (Massey et al. 1993). Within this framework there is a space for both the agency of collectivities and the economic/political structural constraints underpinning them (Goldring 1999). Four initial reasons are advanced to account for the formation of transnational communities: the family reproduction in the face of economic and or political insecurity, social exclusion in the countries of origin, racialised exclusion in countries of reception, active relations between home states and transmigrants (Basch et al. 1994). Moreover, it seems that the importance of status claims in relation to the country of origin reinforces transnational communities, through their investing in their location of origin and their project to reorient regimes of stratification (Goldring 1999). Migrants are simultaneously involved in the country of origin and of reception (Basch et al. 1994) so that a triangular relationship exists (Faist 1999). The neo-liberal organisation of the global economy seems to give states an impetus to create new categories of citizenship facilitating dual belonging (Smith 1999). What is also emphasised is the end of an equation between social space and territorial space: a deterritorialisation of groups takes place (Caglar 1997).

A trend appears to develop whereby ethnic minority groups create transnational communities through an original mobilisation of identity and community resources which enable them to multiply economic and social advantages through their networks. A continuous interaction takes place between their community in the country of origin, the community in the first country of settlement and ramifications of these communities in other countries of settlement. Three stages are identified by Faist (1999): 1) remittances being sent by labour migrants; 2) the birth and growth of ethnic businesses in reception countries; 3) transnational production, distribution and sales. A number of factors are said to make this possible and necessary: economic and/or political exclusion in the society of origin, racialised exclusion in the country of reception (Basch et al. 1994), compounded with the declining legitimacy of cultural assimilation, and the extension of 'multicultural' rights (Goldring 1999) which are seized upon by the migrants through their social capital. This development is apparently enhanced by the global penetration of the neo-liberal model (Smith 1999) but may enable them to cope better than autochthonous populations of the same socioeconomic level. Others have argued that the migrants' situation as strangers and outsiders at the same time as insiders (Simmel 1964), gave them a heightened critical and analytical view of society and that this enabled them to pursue original individual and group strategies.

Social capital is locally based, a 'local asset' and functions as a transmission belt for other forms of capital. Transnational social spaces are said to emerge when persons in distinct places are connected via social and symbolic ties enabling the transfer of various forms of capital; it is grounded in at least two local contexts and has the capacity to link across borders and even continents (Faist 1999). Local assets are thus transformed into international assets through transnational locally based community networks. Two types of transnational-isation are possible: economic and political transnational communities, namely labour migrants and refugees, both evolving through different phases. But in both cases, a process of cumulative causation is observed to explain youth cultures:

> In sum, the feedback processes involving cumulative causation concern a declining legitimacy of cultural assimilation as a shared vision, the extension of 'multicultural' rights, the denial of political rights and the experiences of cultural discrimination and socio-economic exclusion and the translation of cultural and political conflicts from Turkey to Germany and back have contributed to an increasing transnationalisation. (Faist 1999, p. 61)

According to Faist, one is not dealing with a youth subculture with lumpen dimensions and connotations of disintegration. His theoretical approach challenges the notions of disintegration and hybridity, proposing instead a concept of cultural cumulative causation (through an interactive feedback process) and of transnationalised segmented cultural spaces. This accounts for cultural elements from both the sending and receiving countries finding entry in the cultural repertoire whereby a dichotomy appears between the public and private sphere and where multiple ethnic, cultural and religious cleavages exist within the group of migrant origin (Faist 2000).

Conclusion

The history of migration demonstrates that a good share of the migrants will settle even when this was not their initial plan nor the plan envisaged by the policy-makers. This has been verified in all the European countries which were recipients of substantial immigrant groups after World War Two. These populations are now here to stay. Family reunion has taken place and a second/ third generation is growing up on European soil. Their mode of incorporation is further removed from the causes of migration. This is raising sharper issues as they are not immigrants and share the aspirations of their peers of autochthonous origin while they are often caught up in the same process of racialisation as their parents and the discrimination concomitant with it. Education and employment are underlined as main areas of concern both by the young people themselves and by policy makers in majority societies; a third issue is that of racism. The mode of incorporation of this 'second' generation is complex: many remain in the lower strata of society but unlike their parents, cannot call upon a status identification derived from the country of origin. This contributes to a malaise and tensions among those groups. On the other hand, they may also take advantage of resources offered by transnational networks and by their community to improve their situation. Others become assimilated into the majority society. In all three cases, they are part and parcel of the reception society and demand to be treated as such on a par with their more 'autochthonous' peers, even when some wish exists to preserve an ethnic identity. How can the new concepts proposed help to analyse the position of those young people? To mention just a few of the questions discussed above, how does the framework of racism and discrimination affect the young people? How does the categorisation by majority society and self-definition interact in the formulation of their social identity? Do they formulate an ethnic group identification, and/or multiple group identification? What range of strategies do they pursue? Do they partake of transnational social networks and are they 'deterritorialised'? Are they able to call upon a variety of registers and codes?

Chapter Three

Politics and Ethnic Minorities

Introduction

The economic boom of the post-war reconstruction of Britain brought about the arrival of numerous immigrant workers as a response to labour shortages. According to the 1991 Census (Country of Birth, Great Britain) 3.8 million people in Britain were born overseas. However, almost half of these (1.81 million) are from Ireland, Australia, New Zealand, Canada and other countries, including Western Europe. The other 1.96 million were born mostly in New Commonwealth countries and Pakistan.[1] The establishment of ethnic minorities of immigrant origin is a recent phenomenon in Britain which began substantially at the end of the Second World War and in the wake of decolonisation. The implications of this migratory flow had not been foreseen and led to the emergence of laws, policies and changes in the social fabric which are summarised in this chapter.

Immigration and Patterns of Settlement

After the war, the first substantial group of immigrants to Britain came from the Caribbean. In some cases employers had taken steps to recruit Caribbean workers: in 1956, for instance, the London Transport Executive had established liaison with the Barbados Immigrant Services to this effect. Caribbeans who arrived in the 1950s and early 1960s were joined by Indians and Pakistanis in the 1960s. People from the territory that was to become Bangladesh came in the early 1970s. East African Asians came in the early 1970s as a result of victimisation and expulsion (about 2,700 arrived from Uganda in 1972). An estimation of figures for the years 1955–60 demonstrates this. From the total number of 219,540 immigrants, 161,450 came from the Caribbean, 33,070 from India and 17,120 from Pakistan (Rex and Tomlinson 1979). By 1971 the population born in the New Commonwealth had increased to 830,200, and in 1991 the main groups of people born in the New Commonwealth (1,688,396) were the following: 264,591 from the Caribbean, 409,022 from India, 234,107 from Pakistan, 105,012 from Bangladesh, 220,605 from East Africa (mostly originally from the Indian Peninsula), 150,409 from the Far East and 120,659 from Mediterranean countries plus a remainder of 7,479. Moreover it is worth noting that a large proportion of each group came from a few well defined areas of the countries of origin as a result of economic difficulties in the countries concerned (Caribbean, Bangladesh), or political upheavals such as the partition of India and Pakistan which caused vast population displacements in border regions combined with a historical affinity between Sikhs and the Empire (Goulbourne 1991), and specific events like the construction of the Mangla Dam in Azad Kashmir which flooded entire villages in the 1960s; as a consequence, Caribbean people mostly came from Jamaica and Barbados, the majority of Indians came from Punjab and fewer from Gujarat; Bangladeshis in the main came from Sylhet.

The demographic character of these populations has changed considerably over the last 30 years. Immigrants had initially come alone with the intention of returning home after saving sufficient money to buy property in the homeland; in the case of West Indians, sometimes both partners came with this intention, having left children behind. Later on, families became gradually reunited and expanded on British territory, partly as a result of immigration laws which only allowed in close relatives. By 1981 the balance between males and females was almost restored. According to the 1991 Census, out of an estimated 2.6 million people in households with heads born in the New Commonwealth and Pakistan, 1,312,238 were males and 1,323,193 were females, although the discrepancy may prove greater for some groups. One feature of this population is its increasingly 'British born' character: in 1991 about 43.4 per cent were born in Britain. Another aspect is its young age profile with 31 per cent of school age, 23 per cent between 16 and 29, 23 per cent between 30 and 44.

The pattern of settlement of New Commonwealth immigrants throughout Britain was determined by the employment structure which had caused their emigration. They concentrated in the large industrial areas of Britain: in 1991, 58 per cent settled in London and the South East, 18 per cent in the Midlands and 13.2 per cent in the North and North West. These populations were further concentrated within a few areas of the cities where they had settled. This was largely brought about by the structure of the housing allocation market. A residential requirement of three to five years rendered public (Local Authority) housing inaccessible to them in the initial stages of migration, and they could not afford to buy houses in most areas. This led them first to find lodgings, and thereafter to buy, cheap derelict houses, in the most run down area of towns: the inner city. It is also in the inner city that rented accommodation could be found through housing associations, which renovated old properties and rented them out at a reasonable cost. This situation created an effective geographical segregation of New Commonwealth people (Rex and Moore 1967).

Communities and Associations

Chain migration combined with the pattern of settlement to create conditions propitious to the formation of communities. These populations have settled down and are now conscious that they are here to stay. They have begun the long drawn-out process of adaptation (Rex, Joly and Wilpert 1987). As families regrouped, communities were reconstituted with their kinship networks, their institutions, their places of worship, their specific shops and their associations.

In the West Indian communities, men and women generally went out to work and relatively few set up their own businesses. They gathered around local 'Black-led' churches which are broadly called Pentecostal (Goulbourne and Joly 1989). Although they partake more of British culture than Asians, West Indians speak their own form of English, Creole, which was for a long time looked down upon as 'bad English' by teachers in schools.

The Asian communities in Britain display a series of differences based on nation or region of origin and on religion. They speak a variety of languages: among Pakistanis it is Punjabi or a dialect of Punjabi (for Mirpuris from Azad Kashmir) and sometimes Urdu, the national language; among Indians it is in the main Punjabi and Gujarati; people from Bangladesh speak Bengali or a dialect thereof. Several religions are practised by these populations: Islam among Pakistanis, Bangladeshis and some Indians and East African Asians; mostly Hinduism, Buddhism and Sikhism among Indians. They share an extended family system which continues to play an important role in providing emotional and material support.

These communities have given rise to numerous associations, and many of them have set up advice and community centres and supplementary schools. Among people from Pakistan and Bangladesh the main forms of organisation are the mosques. These fulfil multiple functions as places of worship, guardians of values, providers of advice and community services, educational centres (often through their *madrasas* or Koranic schools) and as the pressure group which negotiates with local authorities; they also organise the teaching of the relevant languages (Joly 1987). Among the Indian communities the Indian Workers' Association remained for a long time the only broadly based and active organisation; it is mostly a political class-based organisation and at one time about half of all Punjabi men were said to belong to it (Josephides 1989). It launched a variety of efficient actions and campaigns against racist discrimination and neo-fascist organisations; it also created well attended and militant trade union branches in the factories where its members were working (often in the face of white trade unionist hostility). However, its 'hegemony' has been challenged in later years by organisations supporting an independent Khalistan (in India) based in Sikh temples (Goulbourne 1991).

Ethnic Minorities and Politics

In the early stages of migration, immigrants mostly took an interest in the politics of their country of origin and reproduced the cleavages which obtained there. They created branches of the home parties in Britain such as the People's Party of Pakistan, the Congress Party and the various Indian Marxist parties. Events in the homelands were of great importance and continue to retain interest today among the ethnic communities. The Pakistan Bangladesh war of 1971 fermented hostility among the corresponding communities in Britain. The movement for an autonomous or independent Azad Kashmir finds some supporters in Britain (which led to the foundation of such organisations as the Kashmir Liberation Front) and the debate about Indian controlled Kashmir brought about the killing of the Indian Consul in Birmingham in 1984 by an organisation called the Kashmir Liberation Army. The Khalistani movement in India has aroused an active network of organisations in Britain. The issue of untouchability in India still mobilises groups in Britain. The revival of Islam in the Muslim world found an echo in Britain (although it is by no means the sole nor the principal reason for the multiplication of mosques in Britain). Even events in Tien An Men Square in China aroused a public debate among the Chinese community in Britain, a group which has sometimes been called 'the invisible minority' as it rarely hits the headlines.

However, during the 1980s, the ethnic minorities demonstrated that their principal interest lies in the arena of British politics. The particular historical development of the British Empire and the Commonwealth provided immigrants in Britain with a unique position compared to their counterparts in other European countries. Up until 1983 when the new Nationality Act came into force, any Commonwealth citizen (who was also a British subject) could register as a British citizen after one year of residence in the United Kingdom; this also applied to citizens from Pakistan. These people thus enjoyed the same political and civic rights as British natives: the right to vote and to be elected in local and national elections, the right to serve as jurors and in the armed forces and the right of access to civil service employment. They are supposed to be entitled to all social benefits, can hold trade union responsibilities (when those rights are not thwarted by discrimination) and can form associations without restrictions. Moreover, until 1983, any child born in Britain automatically acquired British citizenship.

As a consequence, in Britain people from the Commonwealth have been able to become involved in mainstream British politics. This is the only case in Europe where large numbers of first-generation immigrants vote, have joined British political parties and are already occupying elected positions: in 1993, there were in Britain at least 250 councillors and six MPs from the ethnic minorities. For a variety of reasons, the majority of people from ethnic minorities vote for the Labour Party although a small minority support the other parties. This pattern remains unaltered whatever the ethnic origin of the candidate. The high concentration of ethnic minority population in small geographical enclaves augments their political clout, as they quite often represent a majority of the electorate in inne city wards and a substantial minority in some parliamentary constituencies (Joly 1988). The Salman Rushdie affair illustrates this situation in Birmingham and Bradford where the Muslim communities have brought considerable pressure to bear on their MPs.

Young People

Parliamentary politics does not encompass all the domains in which ethnic minorities are involved. A number of people from the first generation founded organisations which, albeit active in British politics, have decided to remain outside electoral politics for ideological reasons: they include the Indian Workers' Association mentioned above (but which followed a more institutional path in Southall), the Bangladeshi Workers' Association, the Pakistani Workers' Association, the Kashmiri Workers' Association and some West Indian organisations. These have taken part in a number of broad campaigns in which the main activists have been young people. Although a few young people are beginning to concern themselves with parliamentary politics, and indeed some of them have been elected onto local councils, most of the youths who are politicised join or support other types of movements. These comprise anti-racist campaigns, campaigns against deportations and against immigration laws. Examples are the Campaign against Racist Laws (CARL), Divided

Families Campaigns or Immigration Widows campaigns. Young people are also mobilised on the issue of police violence and arrests, particularly if they result from political activities. Examples include the Newham 7, Mrs Parchment, Colin Roach (killed in police custody), the Bradford 12 and the Smethwick 3. One characteristic of these movements is that they cut across ethnic and religious boundaries, unlike most first-generation based associations, and include both men and women of all origins (Joly 1988). In addition there exist groups of young Asians, such as one formed in Southall to counteract racist and National Front attacks, and Asian or Black women's groups, bringing together young women from various communities. Many young West Indians and Asians were involved in riots in the 1980s. The young Muslims who, barring a few exceptions, had seemed to remain more law-abiding than the rest, were seen to demonstrate virulently on the question of Salman Rushdie. As for young West Indians, a number of them have become Rastafarians. Rastafarianism stays on the margins of British society as it looks towards an eventual return to Africa.

A few general comments need be made at this stage. Young people are confronted with a doubly conflictive situation. On the one hand, they are coming to adulthood in a particularly adverse conjuncture; unemployment and precariousness badly affects the ethnic minorities and the youth suffer from it more than others. While many parents may resign themselves or retreat into their churches and mosques, the young are not ready to take this situation lying down. They feel that they are entitled to as good a treatment as their white peers and resent the discrimination which they experience widely; many of them will say that they are not ready like their parents to accept 'a shit job' (Joly 1989). They are not prepared, either, to tolerate racist abuse and violence without defending themselves. The situation of young West Indians appears to be the worst of all as they are severely affected by unemployment and experience the most damaging relations with the police. Where Asian youths are concerned, more of them, particularly Indians, have done reasonably at school and are therefore equipped with better qualifications. On the other hand, more of the first-generation Asians have set up small businesses, sometimes with redundancy monies from a job they had lost, so that an unemployed Asian youth has more chances of finding some sort of job within the extended family network. Things are changing within the Asian family however. Young couples increasingly set up home on their own, departing from a tradition where the extended family of several generations used to live together. However, the Asian family is undergoing an evolution without collapsing, so that it is still a major source of support (Joly 1989). A more negative element affecting young Muslims is the growth of Islamophobia (CRE 1997).

Immigration Legislation

The 1948 Nationality Act reflected the old ideology of Empire with the notion that Commonwealth and colonial persons shared with British people the common feature of being subjects of the King or Queen. This included the citizens of Australia, New Zealand and Canada, but also the inhabitants of British colonies and ex-colonies which acquired their independence and joined the Commonwealth. Practically all of them did so and formed what is commonly called the New Commonwealth. The Act did establish a distinction between the citizens of the United Kingdom and the colonies, on the one hand, and citizens of the independent Commonwealth, on the other, but allowed all entry to Britain. Thus, when labour shortages became apparent in the wake of the Second World War, there were no legal restrictions on the numbers of colonials and ex-colonials that could be recruited to fill the gap.

However, an opposition to this immigration developed from several quarters, including Conservative politicians and sections of the electorate. It led to the passing of the 1962 Commonwealth Immigration Act, making all entries subject to the holding of employment vouchers. In 1964 vouchers became classified into category A for people with special skills and category B for those with prearranged jobs, and hence more restricted in availability. From then on the trend was set. The Labour Party had originally opposed the introduction of immigration controls but failed to repeal them when it was elected to government in 1964. On the contrary, fear of losing seats to the Conservatives campaigning on an anti-immigration ticket (as happened in Smethwick, Birmingham), seems to have led the Labour Party to change its policy (Rex and Tomlinson 1979). In August 1965, employment vouchers were further reduced to an annual figure of 8,500, and a White Paper presented at the 1965 Labour Party conference proposed further immigration legislation.

In 1968 a new Commonwealth Immigration Act established the principle of *patriality*, which in effect introduced discrimination on a racial basis. This had the aim of subjecting Asians from Africa to immigration controls which had not applied to them until then, as they were full British passport holders. According to the new Act, British passport holders resident in the Commonwealth were only exempted from immigration controls if they had a parent or a grandparent born in Britain (this was likely to mean white people), others were not. In 1969 a ban was imposed on the entry of male fiancés from the Commonwealth who came to get married. In 1971 the Conservative government introduced an Immigration Act which generalised the *patriality* principle, granting the right of abode to *patrials* only, all others having to comply with immigration regulations (i.e. they had to obtain a work permit and register with the police). The Immigration and Asylum Act 1999 further restricted access to Britain with a special focus on asylum seekers (Kelly and Joly 1999).

Finally, the 1981 Nationality Act that came into force in 1983, gave a rational basis to the previous immigration legislation by creating different classes of British citizens: those resident or born in the United Kingdom before 1983, and those living in British protectorates or colonies. The latter do not enjoy any right of abode in Britain. The other major contribution of this Act to British legislation was the abolition of the *jus soli* which had prevailed until then, whereby any child born in Britain had automatically been British whatever the nationality of its parents.

This brief presentation of successive immigration policies demonstrates that from the mid-1960s onwards, the two main parties have in practice agreed on racial discrimination in the area of immigration. This was paralleled and prompted by movements against 'coloured' immigrants from the 1950s onwards. Such attitudes were manifested through racial attacks and acts of discrimination throughout the social spectrum (Josephides 1989). In 1960 associations were set up to oppose immigration, such as the Birmingham Immigration Control Association and the Southall Residents' Association. Politically, popular racism grew in strength and expression, a trend which culminated in Powell's famous speech in April 1968 warning of 'rivers of blood' through the streets of Britain if immigration was not halted and accompanied by deportations. On 23 April, 1,500 dockers marched to Westminster in support of Powell, and later more pro-Powell marches took place in the provinces. In general the trade union movement had been less than favourable to the immigrant workers. This was demonstrated by the joint statement presented by the Trades Union Congress, the Confederation of British Industries and Nationalised Industry to the Minister of Labour in order to oppose the extension of anti-discriminatory legislation to the area of employment. In many areas, for example, the election of shop stewards in trade unions had also resisted ethnic minority membership and representation (Duffield 1988). In the 1970s Powellism was overshadowed by the National Front (NF), a racist and neo-fascist political party, which scored relative electoral successes as illustrated by the following examples. In May 1973

Martin Webster saved his deposit in the West Bromwich by-election, and 26 NF candidates were put up in local council elections in Leicester; in 1977 in the Birmingham Stechford by-election won by Conservatives, the NF candidate beat the Liberal into fourth place (Rex and Tomlinson 1979). In the 1980s both Enoch Powell and the National Front lost their prominence. Racial attacks do continue, however, despite a Home Office investigation into racism.

Race Relations Laws

The foregoing provides a background of many significant measures concerning immigrants and ethnic minorities. It would be misleading, however, to suggest that the adverse immigration laws and attitudes described above express the totality of the complex set of opinions and actions on the issue of ethnic minorities. Indeed, as early as 1950 and again in 1956, private members' bills respectively by the MPs Reginald Sorenson and Fenner Brockway, proposed to outlaw discrimination in public places. They reflected one stream of opinion in the Labour and Liberal Parties to which Labour governments gave expression through varied legislation. Consequently more restrictive immigration laws were generally coupled with measures towards protecting or helping ethnic minorities to integrate (Rex 1988).

One series of laws related to racial discrimination. The first Race Relations Act was passed in October 1965 which outlawed discrimination in public places and incitement to racial hatred. It also set up a Race Relations Board to take action against those infringing the Act and a National Committee for Commonwealth Immigrants (NCCI) to speak in the interest of immigrants. This rather weak piece of legislation was strengthened by the 1968 Race Relations Act which extended its scope to discrimination in the areas of employment and housing. The Race Relations Board was maintained, but the NCCI was replaced by a Community Relations Commission and local Community Relations Councils which shared the vague responsibility of promoting good ethnic relations. The most noticeable impact of these measures was that they contributed to the creation of a large race relations industry of salaried ethnic minority employees; one concomitant effect was to neutralise potentially militant educated immigrants and community leaders (Rex 1988).

The 1976 Race Relations Act covered much broader areas of discrimination, and introduced the concept of indirect discrimination. Under the Act, a newly created Commission for Racial Equality (CRE) was empowered to investigate cases of racial discrimination on an individual basis in firms and in government departments. It could even make recommendations to the Home Office for legal changes it considered necessary for 'good race relations'. The CRE also took over the roles of the Community Relations Commission and the Race Relations Board. Moreover, the 1976 Act called upon local authorities to take on board the question of racial equality (Section 71).

The Development of Social Policy

A third set of policies was developed alongside immigration laws and anti-discrimination legislation; they concerned social policy towards ethnic minorities (i.e. non-legislative action such as the use of statutory instruments, white papers and grants).

Assimilation

Initially the prevalent viewpoint stemmed from an assimilationist ideology and hoped for the elimination of difference and the integration of immigrants into mainstream British society as fast as possible. In education, for instance, it has meant giving exclusive priority to the teaching of English and the recommendation that no school have over 30 per cent immigrant children (Department of Education, circular 7/65, July 1965); in some areas bussing took place as a consequence.

Social Disadvantage

From the mid-1960s onwards, these views were abandoned and the next legislation that specifically addressed ethnic minorities was derived from another outlook: the notion of social disadvantage. The 1966 Local Government Act incorporated a section which made it possible for local authorities to obtain additional funding if they had a substantial number of immigrant residents (Cross et al. 1988). Local authorities themselves appeared to have asked for such provision. It is not clear, however, whether this additional funding was seen as a compensation for what local authorities perceived as an extra burden on services resulting from the presence of immigrants or as a resource destined to benefit the minorities themselves. At any rate the purposes of Section 11 were clarified at a later date (see below). Another manifestation of this underlying 'social disadvantage' outlook was the responsibility of the Community Relations Commission (before it was abolished), conceived to encourage social work initiatives. This approach mostly levels the responsibility for their deprivation at the victims themselves, who are awarded extra social services to deal with their problems (Johnson, Cross and Parker 1981).

This underlying philosophy was further developed when attention was turned to urban deprivation and disadvantage with two successive pieces of policy, neither of which mentioned ethnic minorities. These were subsumed under the 'urban poor' which the 1968 Urban Programme, under the aegis of the Home Office, was supposed to assist. Community Development projects were also initiated to help the disadvantaged. The Urban Programme was reformed and expanded in 1977 following the publication of a White Paper entitled *Policy for the Inner Cities*, which placed it within the remit of the Department of the Environment. Once again ethnic minorities were not mentioned as the principal beneficiaries of these measures. It has been suggested that this could have resulted from the electoral backlash feared by the Labour Party if it was seen to help ethnic minorities. As John Rex says, 'it had to be dealt with by stealth' (Rex and Tomlinson 1979). Moreover, this whole approach made it possible to blame the environment and avoids apportioning responsibilities to the authorities. Inner city urban partnerships comprising the Department of Environment, the Department of Trade and Industry, and central and local government were supposed to achieve a revitalisation of the inner city. However, it remains doubtful whether these measures really benefited ethnic minorities.

Education had not been considered within the inner city policy. Nevertheless, it had come to the attention of the Select Committee on Immigration and Race Relations. As a consequence, a Commission of Enquiry was set up to produce a report on 'the causes of the underachievement of children of West Indian origin'. The Rampton Report, named after the chairman of the Committee, placed the blame for academic failure upon racism in schools on the one hand, and upon the structure of the West Indian community and the family, on the other hand (Troyna 1987). This report provides the harbinger of a growing trend as it begins to identify racism as one factor of disadvantage.

Racial Disadvantage and Communities

The 1980s ushered in new developments in policies for ethnic minorities largely initiated by the minorities themselves. Both parliamentary and extra-parliamentary politics contributed to this. By then it had become apparent that an ethnic minority vote had to be taken into account at least on a local level; the presence of ethnic minority councillors, whose numbers began to grow from the early 1980s, enhanced this realisation. In addition, ethnic minorities had become more densely organised into associations, committees and campaigns. However, the full impact of ethnic minority dissatisfaction and demands was felt when successive urban riots (sometimes referred to as 'uprisings') took place in British inner cities: Bristol in 1980, London (Brixton and Southall), Birmingham (Handsworth), Liverpool (Toxteth), and Manchester (Moss Side) in 1981, and again in the main cities in 1985. A number of reasons account for these events. For ethnic minorities, disadvantage in housing and education was compounded with the recession of the 1970s which hit ethnic minorities more than others, and the young members of these communities most of all. In addition, the racism which had contributed to the creation of skinhead gangs involved in 'Paki bashing', combined with the resentment expressed by young Blacks towards the police, exacerbated the situation in the inner cities. Large numbers of ethnic minority youths perceive the police as racialist and brutal, deliberately harassing and victimising young Blacks; a perception illustrated by the fact that several of the riots were sparked off by police action, and that the organised section of the youth mobilised against racial attacks and racist organisations see the police as protecting aggressors rather than the victims of those attacks.

Police

After 1981 the police came under scrutiny as the Conservative government appointed Lord Scarman, a liberal judge, to examine the question of policing in Brixton. Scarman noted the bad relationship between the police and young West Indians and made a series of recommendations. Despite the moderate tone of these recommendations, they were not accepted either by the government or by the Police Authorities (Rex 1988). If the notion put forward by Scarman of community policing accompanied by consultation with the communities has in some ways been implemented, it does not seem to have altered the situation. It seems that police liaison committees including representatives from the communities did little to prevent the 1985 riots. As for a reforming of police attitudes towards young Blacks, the convictions of policemen for confessions extorted through maltreatment or simply forged by the serious crime squad show that at least in Birmingham little has changed (*Birmingham Post* 16.11.89). In 1999, the Macpherson Report, arising out of the inquiry into Stephen Lawrence's murder, clearly levels accusations of racism at the police institution: 'A central and vital issue which has permeated our Inquiry has been the issue of racism' (p. 20). Eighteen years after the

Scarman Report, racism among the police does not appear to have diminished.

Policy in the 1980s

In the 1980s, policy for ethnic minorities was characterised by a new approach which includes two elements, although these are not always adopted together.

• The notion of 'racial disadvantage' superseded (without altogether eliminating) what had been called the poverty syndrome of ethnic minorities. This led to policies designed to ensure racial equality, i.e. equal opportunity policies, and even sometimes to redress inequality by 'positive action'.
• Cultural identity and difference became fully acknowledged, as was the importance of consulting with communities. Following from this a more recent trend arose towards what is sometimes called 'self help', which is assisting communities and their associations to provide services to ethnic minorities and to develop economic projects.

These two elements are apparent in the next items examined here: education and local authorities.

Education

In 1979 the newly elected Conservative government substituted for the Rampton committee a committee headed by Lord Swann with the brief to examine 'the achievements and needs of all pupils for education for life in a multicultural society' (Troyna 1987). A few comments need to be made here on the two main approaches which have stimulated a sharp debate among educationalists: multiculturalism and anti-racism. Multiculturalism is supposed to make a space for difference and for the specificity of ethnic minority cultures. Thus multicultural teaching would mean the recognition of such cultures and their incorporation into the curriculum. However, the dangers of multi-culturalism, if it is not based within a solid framework of equal opportunity policies, have been highlighted. Indeed, according to Rex, multiculturalism could easily become a vehicle for racial segregation in the absence of such a framework, as in South Africa (Rex 1989). And if multiculturalism was to, as has often been the case, remain limited to inner city schools it could be seen as providing a second-rate substitute for a good academic standard of education. Such multiculturalism has been summed up as 'cultural tourism' or the three Ss: Saris, Samosas and Steel Bands (Troyna 1987). This formula is certain not to satisfy ethnic minority parents and pupils who aspire like others to academic success.

Anti-racism is often counterposed to multiculturalism or posited as a necessary safeguard to it. Anti-racist education is supposed to correct racial disadvantage by submitting the curriculum to sharp scrutiny with a view to eradicate and expose racist prejudice and by making staff and all pupils aware of racism. The Swann Report, *Education for All*, incorporated both multiculturalism and anti-racism in its recommendations. However, it did not endorse the teaching of minority languages. *Education for All* comprised a substantial body of recommendations which were not mandatory. It has been up to the Department of Education and Science (now the Department for Education and Employment), but especially to local education authorities, to implement those. In 1999, discrimination and disadvantage are still characteristic of several ethnic minority groups in the UK (*The Express* 8.3.99, p. 5).

Local Policies from the National to the Local

Laws on racial discrimination have an influence on local authorities and Community Relations Councils created under the 1968 law have played a significant role among local authorities as they remained for a long time the main consultative bodies for municipal decisions concerning ethnic minorities. Moreover, the CRE set up under the 1976 Race Relations Act created local offices in some municipalities which acted as pressure groups. But it was Article 71 of the 1976 Race Relations Act which had the greatest influence as it enabled local authorities to take on the question of equal opportunity. Although it was not taken on board immediately, Article 71 played an important role in the formulation of local authorities' policy in the 1980s.

Measures related to the Urban Programme (1968) complemented by the Inner City Policy Programme (1977) constituted central factors for some local authority action. In 1988, 57 municipalities benefited from this funding which mainly addressed the question of ethnic minorities. Local authorities participate in the management and funding of this programme. Still within the framework of responses to the social handicap which ethnic minorities are deemed to suffer from, the 1966 Local Government Act is particularly significant. It has been argued that Article 11 of the 1966 Act was the very instrument which made it possible for local authorities to apply Article 71 of the 1976 Race Relations Act. Indeed, according to Article 11, local authorities could obtain the funding of an important number of additional posts if they had a set percentage of immigrants. This was limited to localities which had immigrants from the new Commonwealth settled for less than 10 years and funding was not attributed to specific posts or services dealing with the immigrants concerned. The local authority receiving this funding had to take on 25 per cent of salary costs for additional posts. Article 11 was used widely and made it possible to obtain funding as high as £87.5 million in 1986/87, 82 per cent of which was destined for teaching (Home Office Scrutiny of Grant 1988).

In the 1980s it came under criticism from several quarters, including the National Union of Teachers, the government and the ethnic communities, who often asked in what way they benefited from it as it had not yet come to their attention (Cross, Cox and Johnson 1988). As a consequence, Section 11 underwent considerable changes which made it more appropriate to fulfil its role. The 10 years rule was abolished so that Section 11 could address all Commonwealth and Pakistani-born people and their immediate descendants (Circular 72/86). The formula system with unidentified beneficiaries and posts was abolished and replaced by bids for identified posts targeted to ethnic minority needs. An emphasis was laid on consultation with the communities, the local authorities having to show that 'they have consulted the local Commonwealth immigrant community or the local Community Relations Councils' (Cross, Cox and Johnson 1988; Circular 97/1982). Nevertheless it is interesting to note that consultation is required but not acquiescence. After the mid-1980s very few Community Relations Councils (CRCs) had remained the main bodies to be consulted; they had been supplanted by Race Relations Units or ad hoc fora set up by local administrations. The latest Home Office report on Section 11, *A Scrutiny of Grants under Section 11 of the Local Government Act 1966* (December 1988) proposes further modifications, including the removal of the term 'immigrants' and of the limitation to Commonwealth beneficiaries, which excludes people like the Somalis and the Vietnamese. It places a renewed emphasis on consultation and proposes that Section 11 grant should be available direct to voluntary groups in the community (in addition to the current detached duty arrangement). The latter highlights the role of local authorities as facilitators in addition to their other functions and the desire for an increased involvement of the communities in catering for themselves. In 1993, the Local Government (Amendment) Act extended access to Section 11 funding to groups such as refugees who did not originate from the Commonwealth. However, central Government reduced its contribution to Section 11 posts from 75 per cent to 57 per cent with local authorities having to find the remainder. In 1995 a component of Section 11 monies was transferred from the Home Office to the Department of the Environment to be incorporated into the Single Regeneration Budget. Finally, all Section 11 funding ended in 1998.

Where teaching is concerned, no specific law was put in place at national level but special enquiries led to the publication of important reports. After the Rampton Report, the Swann Report, *Education for All* (1985), which examined the achievements and needs of all the pupils for an education which taught them to live in a multicultural society, in turn denounced racism as one of the causes of school underachievement. *Education for All* promoted the incorporation of a multicultural and an anti-racist dimension to teaching. Local authorities responsible for the management of teaching then had to take these recommendations into account.

Ethnic Minority Mobilisation

However, the impact of national measures does not seem to follow a coherent logic. For instance, the principle according to which local authorities had to take on board the question of ethnic minorities according to the 1976 Race Relations Act remained a dead letter until the 1980s. On the other hand the Swann Report (1985) was discussed and taken into account by numerous local authorities as soon as it was published.

Explanations for these contradictions seem to reside in the actions of ethnic minorities themselves, which influenced events at national and local level. Serious and repeated riots in the 1980s which affected numerous towns such as Bristol, Birmingham, Manchester, Liverpool, at the same time as several London boroughs have no doubt shaken local and national government, convincing them that urgent measures about ethnic minorities had to be taken. Moreover, the political participation of minorities and the impact of their roles in local elections could not go unnoticed with local authorities. The election of more than 300 ethnic minority municipal councillors contributed to focus attention on the needs of ethnic communities. For instance, Birmingham in the 1990s counted 21 ethnic minority city councillors out of 117. This meant a third of the Labour group which controlled the municipality (Solomos and Back 1995).

The creation of more numerous and better organised community associations also provided local authorities not only with spokespeople, but with active pressure groups promoting the interest of their members. In some cases this has led to specific measures taken by municipalities for specific groups. For instance, in Birmingham where Muslim communities are numerous and well organised, the Muslim Liaison Committee negotiated with the municipalities a document which includes official recommendations on the cultural and religious needs of Muslim pupils which the local education authority sent to all head teachers. Moreover, some localities became a terrain of confrontation between extreme right-wing organisations and organisations of ethnic minorities. For example, the Indian Workers' Association challenged discrimination in public places during the 1960s and opposed the National Front and the wave of Powellism in the late 1960s and 1970s. Facing these problems, municipalities developed diversified responses which in turn influenced events and policies, constructing a mosaic of specific local situations throughout the country.

The 1990s

If the 1960s and 1970s bore witness to a broadly assimilationist approach from municipalities which was defined nationally, the 1990s were noticeable by qualitative and quantitative changes. On the one hand the question of ethnic minorities came on to the agenda of municipal councils which developed specific policies and created specific structures to implement them. On the other hand, the social/economic approach took second place behind the notion of racial disadvantage while the importance of identity and cultural difference were fully recognised, so that consultation with communities acquired a renewed importance. Along the same line, the concept of self-help was developed under the Conservative government which encouraged communities and their associations to help themselves. This also corresponded with the neo-liberal economic policy introduced by the Conservative government. Current policies adopted by local authorities can be classified into three main categories. Most local authorities embrace all three, but the prominence of each related to the other may vary considerably according to the municipality. Moreover, it is important to distinguish between policies on the one hand (presented below) and on the other hand, their implementation and their impact. The latter may remain far removed from the original goal of the policies or may have unintended consequences ('perverse effects' as they are called in France).

Equal Opportunity

In the main, local authorities have adopted an equal opportunity policy which they implement with regard to employment and services. Municipalities assume an unsuspected importance where employment is concerned as their staff are numerous. For instance, the Birmingham Municipality is the biggest employer in the whole of the West Midland region. Moreover, local authorities can play a normative role on the question of equal opportunity and influence other employers. As for services offered by local authorities, it is more than likely that ethnic minority populations call upon them widely as it is more difficult for them to have access to the private sector because of their social/ economic position (this includes housing, education, health etc.). This policy is implemented through a series of measures destined not only to prevent discrimination in appointments but also to redress existing imbalances. Several authorities measure the composition of their staff according to ethnic criteria and may set the target of a certain percentage of ethnic minority employees. Birmingham, which in 1989 found that 6.9 per cent of employees were of ethnic minority origin, reached 20 per cent in 1997; however, the absolute percentage might not reflect the level of employment at which those groups are appointed. Moreover, positive initiatives may be envisaged to compensate for racial handicap. In Birmingham one proposal was to pursue positive action with regard to employment and training (Race Relations and Equal Opportunities in Birmingham, City of Birmingham 1987).

Communities and Multiculturalism

The second political option available is to take into account the existence of communities and to recognise their specificity; this means a duty to consult them and negotiate with them. Directives issued in 1990 about the application of Article 11 stressed the need to consult with communities and also plan to provide posts for ethnic minority associations. Through the Urban Programme and the Inner City Partnership, funding was released so that associations could set up services destined for their communities. In addition, this policy towards communities includes the recognition and appreciation of differences within the framework of a multicultural approach. Such a political choice also led to services adapted to the specific needs of minorities. In Birmingham, for instance, the Social Services Committee took on the responsibility to ensure that its services were accessible to all the residents who needed them, and that they be adapted as corresponds to the cultural experience of all its users within the scope of available resources (Race Relations and Equal Opportunities in Birmingham, City of Birmingham 1987). In some areas such as education, the community approach led to the introduction of a multicultural programme.

Anti-racism

Several municipalities have introduced in their policies an anti-racist dimension. In order to attain those objectives some municipalities have organised anti-racist training for its staff. In education an anti-racist policy not only means the training of teachers but also the scrutiny of the curriculum and text books. Local authorities have set up a number of structures to implement the policies mentioned above. Their status, their importance and their composition often constitute a good indicator of the degree of importance which local authorities accord the problems of ethnic minorities. These elements also enable one to know which aspects of social policies will be prioritised.

Exclusion, Racism, Partnerships

In the late 1990s, a trend developed towards the establishment of coordinated action against 'inequality, discrimination, social exclusion and all forms of harassment' (Equalities Division Annual Report 1998/99) through the cooperation of a wide range of private, public, voluntary and community organisations. Exclusion and racism have become the two main themes which call upon local authority intervention. 'Cross ethnicity' and the youth are other areas of interest. In Birmingham, two important partnerships have been set up:

• the Birmingham Race Action Partnership aims to insure that Black, Asian and ethnic minority communities have equal access to services, resources and opportunities to influence developments within their local communities;
• the Birmingham Partnership Against Racial Harassment includes the City Council and partner agencies such as West Midlands Police, the Commission for Racial Equality and Birmingham Racial Attacks Monitoring Unit (BRAMU) with other voluntary, statutory and community organisations with the aim of protecting ordinary people from racial harassment and to tackle perpetrators of harassment. It set up a monitoring unit to coordinate support for victims of racial harassment.

Both partnerships state that they are committed to:

- strengthening local ethnic minority communities;
- promoting involvement and participation of socially excluded groups;
- enabling more joined up working between agencies of equality issues;
- accessing resources to support ongoing regeneration within excluded community (Equalities Division Annual Report 1998–99).

In addition, the Birmingham equalities division propose to review fundamentally existing mechanisms for consultation, which entails 'a shift away from the neo-colonial "community leaders" model to one of cross-ethnicity issue based community forum' (EQ Bulletin, January 1999, p. 6).

Conclusion

British society has undergone profound changes since the arrival of labour migrants to meet the needs of expanding economies after the Second World War. Not only is it clear that these populations are here to stay but the state has had to respond to their presence and their demands in British society. Policies regarding ethnic minorities have evolved in an ad hoc way and often with unintended consequences: for example, certain measures have followed from previous ones either resulting in a 'snowball effect' of legislation and directives or, conversely, in a pulling back from the status quo depending on the balance of forces at play; their implementation follows the same uneven pattern. Undoubtedly this field has expanded and one even speaks today of a 'race relations industry' to refer to this package of institutionalised measures. In the UK, assimilationist initiatives gave way to policies addressing social disadvantage while the mid-1980s saw the introduction of a three-pronged approach including equal opportunity (to counter 'racial disadvantage'), community/cultural recognition and anti-racism. More recently an anti-exclusion approach has been introduced. These approaches are most strongly manifested at local level, where they are adopted together or separately in varying degrees (Joly 1995). Throughout the last 30 years the policies proposed have evolved but none so far has achieved satisfactory outcomes.

From a labour force of people keeping their cultural identity private, immigrant groups have evolved into communities with a rich complex of networks, institutions and associations. Ethnic minority groups are participating in the political process and have mobilised to further their demands and defend their interests: in the mainstream political parties, in the organisations of civil society, in their own associations and sometimes in the streets, as evidenced by the urban riots of the 1980s. They are the main driving force behind changes in the state management of their integration. Young people of ethnic minority origin are creating a space for themselves in this changing social fabric, compounded by neo-liberal economic policies prevalent in Britain.

Note

1   This includes: in Eastern Africa, Kenya, Malawi, Tanzania, Uganda, Zambia; in Southern Africa, Botswana, Lesotho, Swaziland. Zimbabwe; in Western Africa, Gambia, Ghana, Nigeria, Sierra Leone; in the Caribbean, Barbados, Jamaica, Trinidad and Tobago, Antigua, Saint Kitts-Nevis, Anguilla, Belize, Guyana; in South Asia, Pakistan, Bangladesh, India, Sri Lanka; in South East Asia, Hong Kong, Malaysia, Singapore; on the Mediterranean, Cyprus, Gibraltar, Malta including Gozo; and others such as Mauritius, Seychelles, Falkland Islands and various Pacific territories.

Chapter Four

Minority Ethnic Groups in Birmingham

David Owen

Introduction

Birmingham lies at the heart of the second largest urban agglomeration in Great Britain and around a million people now live within the administrative boundary of the city. Together with London, the city (and the wider West Midlands conurbation) was the first destination of migrants from the New Commonwealth arriving in the United Kingdom in the immediate post-Second World War decades. It still has the second largest concentration of people from minority ethnic groups in Great Britain, who formed 23 per cent of the city's population (231,000 people) at the time of the 1991 Census. The minority ethnic group population of Birmingham is thus larger and more concentrated than anywhere else in Britain, with the exception of a number of London Boroughs. The city's minority population continues to grow, mainly due to a relatively high birth rate in a youthful population, augmented by migration into the city, though this is now running at a much slower rate than in the 1950s and 1960s.

This chapter presents information on the ethnic composition of Birmingham, how this varies within the city and how the ethnic composition of the city is very different for different age groups. In parts of the city the population from minority ethnic groups now outnumbers the white population and minority ethnic groups are forming an increasing proportion of the child population. The chapter draws upon information from a range of sources in order to illustrate the differences between ethnic groups in terms of their experience in the labour market and the education system and also presents limited information on patterns of crime and offending behaviour by ethnic group.

Ethnic Composition of the City

The most comprehensive information on the social and economic characteristics of the British population is that collected by the decennial Census of

Population. This is also the only source of population information for small areas. The 1991 Census was the first to collect information on the ethnic background of the population, and thus it provides the benchmark data for this chapter.

Table 1 details the ethnic breakdown of the population of Birmingham in 1991, using the tenfold ethnic group classification adopted by the Office for National Statistics. Minority ethnic groups made up nearly a quarter of the city's population, with three-fifths of the minority population coming from the three South Asian ethnic groups (Figure 1). A further 30 per cent were from the three Black ethnic groups. There were three large minority ethnic groups in the city; Pakistani people, who alone comprised 30 per cent of the minority population, Indian and Black-Caribbean people, the latter two each accounting for just under a quarter of the minority population. The Black-Other and Other-Other ethnic groups each accounted for around 5 per cent of all people from minority ethnic groups. Both of these ethnic groups include people of mixed parentage, but the former also includes people with Black-Caribbean or Black-African parents who would prefer to describe themselves as being 'Black-British', while the latter includes a range of less populous ethnic groups (such as Arabs and Iranians) as well as people who could not easily be classified into any of the other ethnic groups.

Males outnumbered females in each minority ethnic group, in contrast to the white population, in which females were in the majority. The greatest gender imbalance occurred in the Black-African ethnic group, in which there were nearly 40 per cent more males than females, followed by the Chinese ethnic group, in there were 20 per cent more males than females. The reason for this imbalance probably lay in the difference in age structure between ethnic groups. The white population was much older on average (see below), and since women have a longer life expectancy than men, they comprised a larger percentage of the population.

Just over half the minority population living in Birmingham in 1991 had been born in the UK. Those people most likely to have been born abroad were from the Chinese, Other-Asian, Bangladeshi and Black-African ethnic groups. All of these had more recent migration histories (and included more overseas students) than the Black-Caribbean, Indian and Pakistani ethnic groups. There was a major contrast between all these ethnic groups and the two 'Other' categories, in which the great majority of people had been born in the UK. There are two reasons for this; because the Black-Other category includes people who identified themselves as 'Black British' and because both categories include people of mixed parentage.

Table 1   Ethnic composition of Birmingham in 1991

Ethnic group	Population	% of total	Males per 1,000 females	% born in the UK	% with long-term illness
White	768,812	76.9	935	94.2	15.2
Minority ethnic groups	*230,833*	*23.1*	*1,098*	*54.4*	*9.7*
Black ethnic groups	*68,571*	*6.9*	*1,099*	*63.2*	*11.0*
Black-Caribbean	3,452	0.3	1,370	44.7	10.6
Black-African	54,359	5.4	1,088	58.3	12.1
Black-Other	10,760	1.1	1,073	94.1	6.0
South Asian ethnic groups	*139,771*	*14.0*	*1,093*	*50.2*	*9.5*
Indian	54,871	5.5	1,075	50.9	9.1
Pakistani	71,138	7.1	1,106	51.5	9.5
Bangladeshi	13,763	1.4	1,095	40.2	11.0
Chinese and other ethnic groups	*22,491*	*2.2*	*1,129*	*56.7*	*7.2*
Chinese	3,638	0.4	1,186	25.8	4.7
Other-Asian	6,237	0.6	1,106	34.8	8.2
Other-Other	12,616	1.3	1,124	76.3	7.5
All ethnic groups	**999,646**	**100**	**970**	**85.7**	**14.0**

Source: 1991 Census of Population (Crown Copyright), adjusted for the 'undercount'.

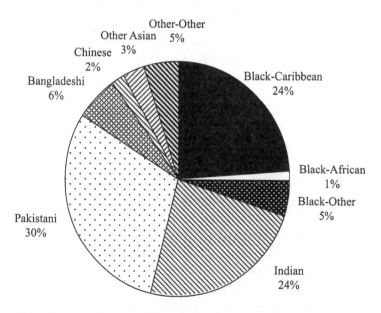

Figure 1   Shares of the minority ethnic group population of Birmingham in 1991 by ethnic group

Contrasts in health between individual ethnic groups can be indicated by the percentage suffering from a long-term (lasting more than a year) limiting illness. The percentage of people with a long-term illness was much smaller for people from minority ethnic groups than for white people, but this crude comparison is complicated by the difference in age structure between ethnic groups. The percentage of older people is much higher in the white than in the minority population (Table 2), and older people are much more likely than younger people to suffer from long-term health problems. Nevertheless, it is possible to compare individual minority ethnic groups, as their age structures are more similar to each other. This reveals the highest percentage of illness for Black ethnic groups, particularly Black-Caribbean people, and Bangladeshi people, lower illness rates for Indian and Pakistani people and the lowest illness rates of all for Chinese people. The Bangladeshi, Black-Other and Other-Other ethnic groups are very youthful, and hence rates of illness among older people are probably higher than the figures in Table 1 indicate. Given that the Bangladeshi illness rate is already one of the higher rates among the minority ethnic groups, this may indicate that people from this ethnic group suffer poorer health than those from other minority ethnic groups.

Table 2 demonstrates contrasts in age structure between ethnic groups. Clearly, people from minority ethnic groups were on average much younger than white people; the percentage of children was twice as high in the minority population as the white population, while the percentage of pensionable age was five times higher for white people, and the percentage in the pre-retirement age group was one-and-a-half times that for minority ethnic groups. Among minority ethnic groups, the most youthful were the Black-Other and Other-Ethnic groups, half of the population of which had not yet reached minimum school leaving age. Nearly two-thirds of Pakistani and Bangladeshi people were aged under 25. In contrast, the highest percentages of people aged from 45 to retirement age and of pensionable age occurred in the Black-Caribbean and Indian ethnic groups, followed by the Chinese ethnic group.

Consequently, the ethnic composition of the population varied considerably by age group (Table 3). Among those of pensionable age, over 94 per cent of the population was white. However, at the other extreme, more than a third of children aged 0–4 and over a third of school age children were from minority ethnic groups. The percentage of the population from minority ethnic groups diminished with increasing age. This decline was faster for the South Asian groups, which made up a fifth to a quarter of the residents of the city aged under 25 and slower for Black people, amongst whom Black-Caribbean people made up the largest part of the minority population of pensionable age. Among

children and young people, Pakistanis were the largest minority ethnic group, while the number of people from the Other-Other and Black-Other ethnic groups was increasing and already greater than the number of Bangladeshi people.

Population Change During the 1990s

Overall, the population of Birmingham grew very slightly (by 0.7 per cent) between 1991 and 1998, but this obscures a shift in the ethnic composition of the population, revealed through a comparison of 1991 data with estimates of the population by age and ethnic group for 1998 (Table 4). The white ethnic group is estimated to have lost more than 2 per cent of its population, while the number of people from minority ethnic groups is estimated to have increased by nearly a sixth (11.1 per cent). The Black ethnic groups as a whole gained population more slowly than the South Asian and 'Chinese & Other' ethnic groups. The Black-Caribbean, Indian and Chinese ethnic groups grew relatively slowly, while the Pakistani and Bangladeshi ethnic groups each increased by around a sixth over this seven year period. The fastest rates of growth of all occurred in the Black-Other and Other-Other ethnic groups, each of which increased in size by more than a quarter.

There was also a more complex pattern of change for individual age groups. The general ageing in the population can be seen in the growth in the number of people aged 25 to 44 and from 45 to retirement age, but the number of people of pensionable age declined. The impact of the 'demographic time-bomb'[1] can be seen in the decline of more than a tenth in the number of young adults (aged 16 to 24), and the number of preschool age children also declined. The most rapid increase was in the number of people aged from 5 to 15.

The decline in the number of pre-school age children affected the white ethnic group most severely, with the number of 0–4 year olds an eighth smaller in 1998 than 1991. The number of Black-Caribbean, Black-African and Chinese children in this age group also declined, but the growth in the number of 'Black British' and 'mixed parentage' children is estimated to have continued, with the Black-Other and Other-Other ethnic groups each increasing by about a quarter. The continued rapid growth of the Bangladeshi and Pakistani ethnic groups is demonstrated by the increase of nearly a fifth and over a sixth respectively, in the number of 0–4 year olds from these ethnic groups.

In contrast, the percentage increase in 5 to 15 year olds was faster for the white ethnic group than for minority ethnic groups as a whole. Amongst these,

Table 4   Estimated population change between 1991 and 1998 for Birmingham: percentage change in the population of each age group

Ethnic group	All ages	0–4 year olds	5–15 year olds	16–24 year olds	25–44 year olds	45–retirement age	Pensionable age
White	-2.3	-12.1	12.1	-18.8	-0.5	3.6	-8.2
Minority ethnic groups	*11.1*	*11.1*	*4.0*	*8.7*	*22.0*	*5.3*	*69.8*
Black	8.2	5.6	18.3	-13.1	22.9	-22.3	68.5
Black-Caribbean	4.1	-3.9	10.4	-21.1	19.6	-25.3	67.5
Black-African	5.7	-4.0	2.9	-18.6	9.4	23.5	97.3
Black-Other	29.6	23.6	41.3	21.0	54.8	22.3	92.2
South Asian	*11.4*	*12.1*	*-3.6*	*16.5*	*21.6*	*20.5*	*71.5*
Indian	6.7	1.3	-7.9	0.4	10.8	38.3	40.2
Pakistani	14.2	16.4	-1.8	23.6	31.2	12.1	94.4
Bangladeshi	16.3	19.1	-0.5	44.3	37.1	-9.9	204.6
Chinese and other	*17.5*	*16.4*	*26.3*	*10.4*	*21.2*	*22.4*	*65.5*
Chinese	3.6	-8.9	5.5	-40.2	24.0	16.4	41.9
Other-Asian	9.6	1.0	7.1	-1.0	9.3	45.4	85.8
Other-Other	25.5	23.1	36.2	38.3	28.9	8.5	69.1
All ethnic groups	**0.7**	**-4.2**	**9.1**	**-10.8**	**4.4**	**3.9**	**-3.9**

Source: CRER estimates of population change based on the Census and ONS estimates of the 1998 population.

the number from the Black-Other ethnic group increased by two-fifths, with a slightly slower rate of increase for the Other-Other ethnic group. The number of South Asian children in this age range declined slightly, but there were increases for the Black-Caribbean, Chinese and Other-Asian ethnic groups.

The number of white young adults declined by nearly a fifth, while the total number of young people from minority ethnic groups increased by a tenth during this period, thus resulting in a marked shift in the ethnic composition of people participating in further and higher education and entering the labour market for the first time. Turning to individual ethnic groups, the largest increases occurred in the Bangladeshi, Other-Other, Pakistani and Black-Other ethnic groups. The number of young Indian adults hardly changed, while there were estimated to be a marked decline in the number from the Black-Caribbean ethnic group (and also the Chinese and Black-African ethnic groups; though inmigration of students might counterbalance this trend for these ethnic groups).

The number of people aged 25 to 44 and from 45 to retirement age increased in most minority ethnic groups, though there was a fall in the number of Black-Caribbean and Bangladeshi people in the older age group, since many people from the migrant generation were reaching retirement age. Over this period, the number of people of retirement age from minority ethnic groups is estimated to have increased by two-thirds, and doubled (Pakistanis) or even trebled (Bangladeshis) in individual ethnic groups, while the number of white people in this age group declined slightly.

The overall change in the share of the population from minority ethnic groups over this period is depicted in Figure 2. Overall, minority ethnic groups represented almost a quarter (24.4 per cent) of the city's population in 1998, while their share of preschool age children had risen from 34 per cent to 39.4 per cent. The minority share of the population increased markedly in all age groups except 5–15 year olds (in which there was a slight decline) and people aged from 45 to retirement age. The minority share of all people of pensionable age almost doubled between 1991 and 1998.

Economic Characteristics by Ethnic Group

Differences in prosperity between ethnic groups are reflected through their involvement in the labour market. The percentage of men aged 16 and over economically active (either working or looking for work) was highest for the Black-Other, Black-Caribbean and Indian ethnic groups and lowest for

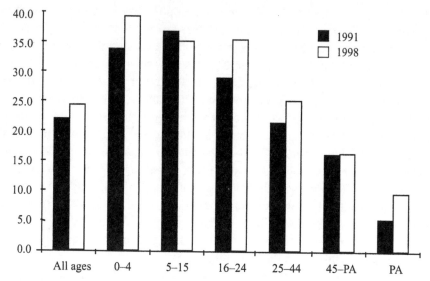

Figure 2 **Percentage of Birmingham's population from minority ethnic groups in 1991 and 1998**

Source: CRER estimates of population change based on the Census and ONS estimates of the 1998 population.

the Bangladeshi and Chinese ethnic groups. Contrasts in economic activity are even greater for women; while two-thirds of Black-Caribbean women aged 16 and over were active in the labour market, only a fifth of Pakistani and Bangladeshi women were economically active. The percentage of white people economically active is lower than for people from minority ethnic groups, because the percentage of people of pensionable age (and thus mainly retired) is much higher for the white ethnic group.

Two indicators of disadvantage (and hence possibly discrimination) in the labour market are the percentage of an ethnic group in work and the unemployment rate (the percentage of the economically active out of work). For people from minority ethnic groups, the former was lower for people from minority ethnic groups than for white people, while the latter measure was higher for people from minority ethnic groups. Just over half of men from the Chinese and Black ethnic groups were in work, but under half of Pakistani men and just over third of Bangladeshi men were in work. Given that Bangladeshi people earn less than other ethnic groups (Owen et al., 2000; Modood et al., 1997), this is an indication of the poverty faced by this ethnic group. In contrast, nearly two-thirds of Indian men (a higher fraction than for white men) were in work. Overall, only a third of women from minority ethnic groups were in work, but the percentage of Black women in work was similar to that of Black men. The low attachment of Pakistani and Bangladeshi women to the labour market is again demonstrated by the very low percentage in work (under an eighth of all women, compared with just under half of Indian women).

There are also marked variations between ethnic groups in unemployment rates faced by all workers and by economically active young people (aged 16 to 24). Amongst men, the unemployment rate for all men from minority ethnic groups was double that for the white ethnic group, though the differential was slightly smaller for young men. Only for the Chinese and Indian ethnic groups was the overall male unemployment rate under 20 per cent, with more than a quarter of Black men out of work. Over a third of Pakistani and over two-fifths of Bangladeshi men were unemployed. However, there was less variation in youth unemployment rates, with around 40 per cent of young men from each minority ethnic group unemployed, with the main exception being the lower unemployment rates faced by Chinese (20 per cent – just less than the white unemployment rate) and Indian (29.1 per cent) young men.

Unemployment rates for women from most ethnic groups were lower than those for men, with the exception of Pakistani and Bangladeshi women, nearly half of whom were unemployed. Unemployment rates for Black, Indian and Chinese women were similar, at around twice the percentage of white women unemployed. The percentage of young women from minority ethnic groups as a whole unemployed was about 50 per cent higher than that for all economically active women from minority ethnic groups, and nearly 2.5 times the corresponding white unemployment rate. However, the percentage of Chinese young women unemployed was less than that of white women. More than a quarter of young Black women were unemployed, and unemployment rates for Pakistani and Bangladeshi young women were well above those of young men from these ethnic groups, at around two-fifths of the economically active.

Another perspective on income differentials is provided by Platt and Noble (1999), who used housing benefit data to identify income contrasts between ethnic groups in Birmingham (Table 6). More than half of Bangladeshi households living in the city were in receipt of housing or council tax benefit, double the average for all households. The percentage of Black households receiving these benefits was just above average, while the corresponding percentage for Pakistani households was double that for white households. This again demonstrates the low incomes of Pakistani households and the extremely disadvantaged position of Bangladeshi people.

**Table 5   Percentage of households from low-income ethnic groups
in receipt of housing benefit**

Ethnic group of	% of 1991 population receiving Income Support and Housing or Council Tax benefit	% of 1991 population receiving Housing or Council Tax benefit and Income Support	% receiving Housing or Council Tax benefit
Bangladeshi	45.1	11.3	56.4
Black Afro-Caribbean and Black-Other	21.6	8.1	29.7
Pakistani	32.6	8.6	41.2
White	14.2	7.2	21.4
Total benefit population	**19.7**	**8.6**	**28.3**

Source: Platt and Noble, 1999, p. 23.

Geographical Distribution of Ethnic Groups

In broad terms, the minority population of Birmingham is predominantly located in the inner part of the city, mainly on the western side of the city centre. Figure 3 depicts the percentage of the population from each of the three broad groupings of minority ethnic groups (Black, South Asian and 'Other') within the 39 electoral wards in Birmingham.

There is a ring of wards surrounding the city centre with high percentages of the population from minority ethnic groups. In most of these, the largest component of the minority population was the South Asian ethnic groups, making up around half the population in Sparkhill, Small Heath and Sparkbrook wards. The Black ethnic groups were much more concentrated on the western side of the city, accounting for their largest shares of the population (nearly a quarter) in Handsworth, Aston and Soho wards. Overall, in Handsworth, Small Heath, Sparkbrook and Sparkhill, over two-thirds of the population was from minority ethnic groups. The minority share of the population in southern wards is much smaller, and their share is even smaller in the northern part of the city.

Figure 4 illustrates the even greater percentages of children from minority ethnic groups. The geographical pattern is broadly similar, but the minority share of the population was larger in most wards, even where minority population shares were small, in the north and south of the city.

In Soho, Sparkbrook, Sparkhill and Small Heath, more than three-quarters of 0–15 year olds were from minority ethnic groups, and more than half were

Table 6   Economic characteristics of ethnic groups in Birmingham, 1991

Ethnic group	Men					Women		
	% aged 16+ economically active	% working	Unemployment rate	Youth unemployment rate	% aged 16+ economically active	% working	Unemployment rate	Youth unemployment rate
White	71.4	60.8	14.9	20.9	47.8	43.8	8.2	13.7
Minority ethnic groups	74.2	53.6	27.7	36.1	46.0	36.1	21.4	32.1
Black ethnic groups	77.5	56.0	27.7	39.0	65.5	54.6	16.6	28.3
Black-Caribbean	77.5	56.5	27.2	39.5	66.1	55.6	15.9	28.3
Black-African	66.9	48.4	27.7	42.2	59.3	47.6	19.7	29.3
Black-Other	84.2	57.0	32.2	36.7	63.0	49.6	21.3	27.7
South Asian ethnic groups	73.2	52.7	27.9	34.5	35.6	26.3	26.1	34.7
Indian	76.3	62.4	18.3	29.1	52.4	43.7	16.6	22.2
Pakistani	71.7	46.4	35.3	38.8	22.0	12.1	44.8	47.2
Bangladeshi	64.9	37.9	41.5	29.9	21.0	11.8	44.0	38.9
Chinese and other ethnic groups	70.4	52.2	25.9	38.2	45.5	35.4	22.2	28.9
Chinese	59.8	50.6	15.5	20.0	42.0	36.0	14.3	11.9
Other-Asian	69.7	49.2	29.4	42.9	42.4	30.9	27.2	38.5
Other-Other	75.8	54.9	27.6	40.5	49.4	38.4	22.2	29.0
Born in Ireland	63.4	48.1	24.1	32.6	43.7	39.4	9.8	18.0
All ethnic groups	**71.9**	**59.5**	**17.2**	**24.3**	**47.5**	**42.5**	**10.4**	**17.7**

Source: 1991 Census of Population (Crown Copyright).

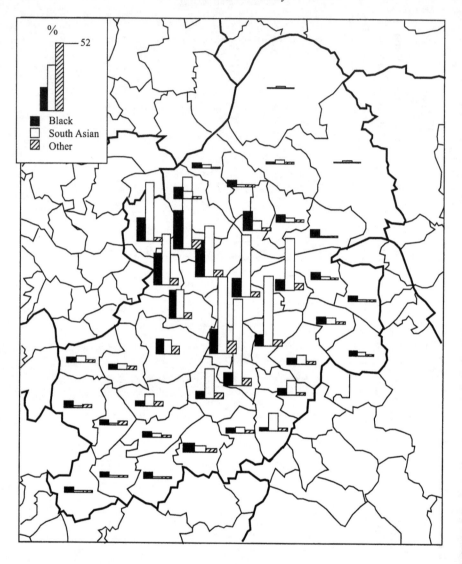

Figure 3   Distribution of people of all ages from minority ethnic groups, 1991

Source: 1991 Census of Population (Crown Copyright), adjusted for the 'undercount'.

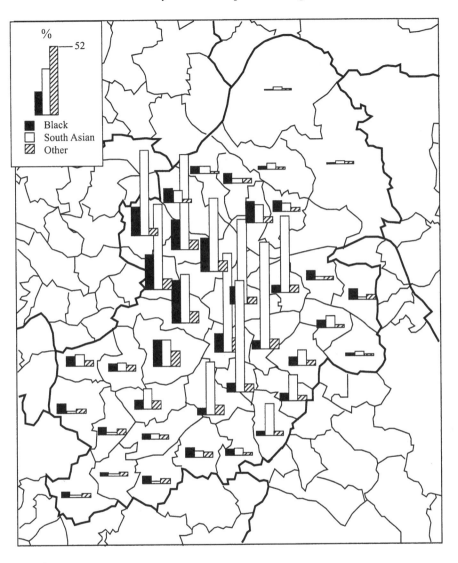

**Figure 4   Distribution of children (aged 0 to 15) from minority
ethnic groups, 1991**

Source: 1991 Census of Population (Crown Copyright), adjusted for the 'undercount'.

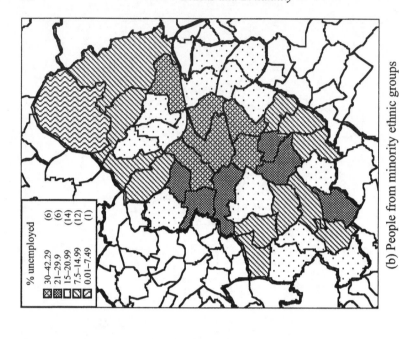

(b) People from minority ethnic groups

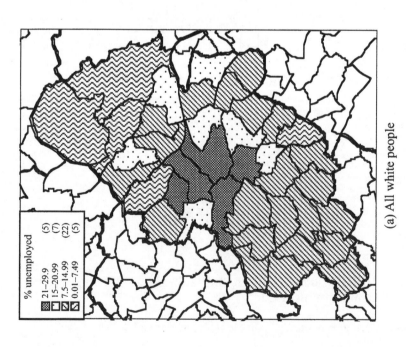

(a) All white people

Figure 5   Unemployment rates by electoral ward, 1991

Source: 1991 Census of Population Local Base Statistics (Crown Copyright; ESRC purchase).

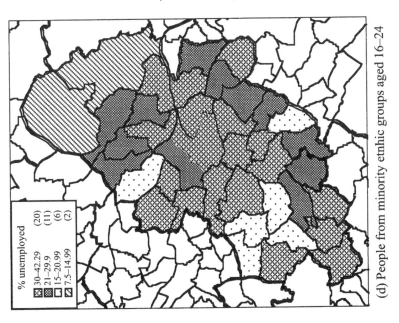

% unemployed

30–42.29　(20)
21–29.9　(11)
15–20.99　(6)
7.5–14.99　(2)

(d) People from minority ethnic groups aged 16–24

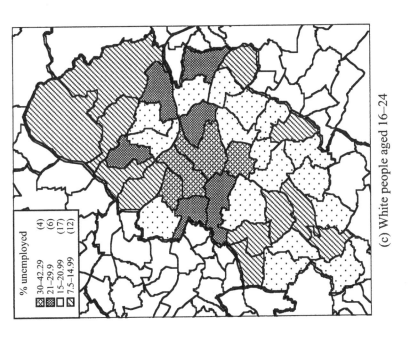

% unemployed

30–42.29　(4)
21–29.9　(6)
15–20.99　(17)
7.5–14.99　(12)

(c) White people aged 16–24

South Asian. In Small Heath, two-thirds of children were South Asian. However, in many wards, including Handsworth, the percentage of children from Black ethnic groups was lower than the percentage of all persons from minority ethnic groups. Black children were also more likely to live on the western side of the city centre.

Geographical Variations in Unemployment

Unemployment rates for white people and people from minority ethnic groups for all ages and for the 16 to 24 age group are presented in Figures 5(a) to 5(d), based on data from the 1991 Census of Population (unfortunately, there is no more up-to-date source of comparable information). All four maps show the same basic pattern of highest unemployment rates in the city centre, low unemployment rates in the north of the city around Sutton Coldfield, and intermediate rates of unemployment in the southern half of the city.

However, people from minority ethnic groups experienced higher rates of unemployment than white people across the whole of the city, and higher unemployment in the southern wards (e.g. King's Norton). Unemployment rates for young people were much higher than the average across all wards, but young people from minority ethnic groups experienced extremely high unemployment rates in all parts of the city. In 31 out of 39 wards, more than 21 per cent of economically active people aged 16 to 24 were out of work, and in half the city's wards, more than 30 per cent were unemployed. These very high unemployment rates occurred in a much wider ring of wards around the city centre and in the Longbridge/King's Norton area in the south of the city. Only in the northern wards of the city were less than 15 per cent of young people unemployed.

Housing and Households

There were considerable differences in household structure and housing conditions between ethnic groups in 1991. Table 7 demonstrates that households whose head was from a minority ethnic group, especially one of the South Asian ethnic groups or born in the New Commonwealth, were substantially larger than white households, with Bangladeshi and Pakistani households the largest of all. However, Black households were similar in size to white households. The main factor underlying differences in household

Table 7　Households and housing by ethnic group, 1991

Ethnic group or country of birth of household head	Household size		Percentage of households						
	Mean no. persons per household	Dependent children per household	Pensioner	Single adult	Lone parent family	Large families	Owner occupiers	Social renters
White	2.3	0.5	27.9	13.9	4.9	4.6	59.9	32.3
Minority ethnic groups	*3.7*	*1.5*	*4.5*	*15.1*	*11.2*	*18.3*	*61.1*	*30.0*
Black	*2.5*	*0.8*	*7.4*	*26.4*	*19.3*	*5.1*	*42.8*	*49.8*
Black-Caribbean	2.5	0.7	8.0	25.7	18.6	5.2	44.2	49.2
Black-African	2.7	1.0	4.6	31.5	13.7	7.3	37.6	46.0
Black-Other	2.5	1.0	1.8	31.2	31.1	2.6	30.2	59.5
South Asian	*4.8*	*2.1*	*2.4*	*5.4*	*4.5*	*30.1*	*78.4*	*13.2*
Indian	4.3	1.6	3.5	6.0	3.6	26.6	83.6	10.0
Pakistani	5.2	2.5	1.5	5.3	5.1	32.4	77.2	13.3
Bangladeshi	5.7	3.0	1.8	3.0	5.2	36.5	57.6	29.9
Chinese and other	*3.3*	*1.3*	*3.6*	*18.4*	*12.5*	*11.8*	*47.0*	*34.9*
Chinese	3.1	1.0	6.5	15.4	5.3	14.0	51.7	25.8
Other-Asian	3.9	1.6	1.6	11.9	5.7	18.6	54.3	28.1
Other-Other	3.0	1.2	3.5	23.1	19.1	7.2	41.2	42.4
All	**2.5**	**0.6**	**24.6**	**14.1**	**5.8**	**6.6**	**60.1**	**32.0**
Head born in the New Commonwealth	4.0	–	23.1	–	–		70.4	22.1
Head born in Ireland	2.4	0.4	23.1	16.6	3.2	6.9	52.3	39.0

Source: 1991 Census of Population Local Base Statistics (Crown Copyright; ESRC purchase).

size was differences in the average number of dependent children (aged 0 to 18). In Bangladeshi households, there were on average three dependent children, six times as many as in white households. White and Black-Caribbean households contained the fewest dependent children, on average.

Small households were more typical of white and Black households than South Asian households. A quarter of white households contained only pensioners and a further eighth contained a single adult of less than pensionable age. Less than 5 per cent of minority households were pensioner households, but nearly an eighth comprised lone parent families, compared with under 5 per cent of white households. These were most characteristic of Black households, with a fifth of Black-Caribbean and nearly a third of Black-Other households being lone parent families. The percentage of lone parent families was slightly higher than for white people in the Pakistani, Bangladeshi, Chinese and Other-Asian ethnic groups, while a fifth of 'Other-Other' households comprised lone parent families. In contrast, more than a third of Pakistani and Bangladeshi households and a quarter of Indian households comprised large families (three or more adults plus dependent children). In the white and Black ethnic groups, this category accounted for only one in 20 households (with the exception of Black-Africans), while the percentage of large families among Chinese and Other-Asian households was rather higher.

There was little difference between white people and minority ethnic groups as a whole in the percentage of households owning their own accommodation and renting from social landlords (the local authority or a housing association). However, Black and Other-Other people were much less likely than average to own, and much more likely to rent from social landlords (this being most marked for Black-Other people, among whom three-fifths were social renters). Indian and Pakistani people were most likely to own their own accommodation, with only an eighth of households living in social rented accommodation. The remainder of the population lived in private rented accommodation, which was most significant for Chinese, Other-Asian and Black-African households (a relatively high percentage of whom are students). Households with heads born in the New Commonwealth were more likely than average to own their own homes, while those with heads born in Ireland were less likely than average to own their own homes and more likely to rent from social landlords.

Table 8 presents three commonly-used measures of living conditions for households from each ethnic group. A household is defined as living in overcrowded conditions if there is more than one person to each room (excluding the kitchen and bathroom) in the dwelling. Clearly, larger households are more likely to live in overcrowded conditions than small households. Thus, people living in households whose head is from a minority ethnic group were six times more likely than people living in white-headed households to live in overcrowded conditions in 1991. Overcrowding was most severe for South Asian households, with more than half of all Bangladeshi people and nearly half all Pakistani people living in overcrowded conditions in 1991. In other ethnic groups, overcrowding was most severe for Indian, Other-Asian, Other-Other and Black-African people. People from the other Black ethnic groups, whose household size was smaller, were less likely to live in overcrowded conditions.

Table 8   Living conditions by ethnic group, 1991

		Percentage of population living in:		
Ethnic group or country of birth of household head	overcrowded households	households lacking amenities	non self-contained households	households without a car
White	4.9	1.0	0.5	35.4
Minority ethnic groups	*30.0*	*1.1*	*0.5*	*42.1*
Black	*9.4*	*0.8*	*0.7*	*55.9*
Black-Caribbean	8.9	0.7	0.6	55.6
Black-African	16.0	1.0	1.9	49.8
Black-Other	11.4	1.3	1.1	62.7
South Asian	*39.6*	*1.2*	*0.3*	*36.5*
Indian	25.5	0.7	0.2	22.6
Pakistani	47.1	1.6	0.4	41.2
Bangladeshi	56.8	1.1	0.2	67.8
Chinese and other	*21.6*	*1.3*	*1.0*	*40.6*
Chinese	14.9	1.8	1.3	29.1
Other-Asian	26.8	0.5	0.7	33.8
Other-Other	20.6	1.7	1.2	50.3
All	**10.2**	**1.1**	**0.5**	**36.8**
Head born in the New Commonwealth	32.4	1.0	0.3	38.4
Head born in Ireland	6.9	1.5	1.2	47.7

Source: 1991 Census of Population Local Base Statistics (Crown Copyright; ESRC purchase).

Another indicator of deprivation is lack of basic amenities such as a bathroom or WC. Very few households lacked these amenities in 1991. While people from the Black-Caribbean, Indian and Other-Asian ethnic groups were more likely than white people to live in housing which had such amenities (perhaps because social housing is more likely than privately owned housing to have these), the percentage of Chinese, Other-Other and Pakistani people living in housing without these amenities was somewhat higher than for other ethnic groups. Black-African, Chinese, Other-Other and Black-Other people were most likely to live in accommodation which was not self-contained, reflecting the higher percentage of households in the private rented sector in housed in shared occupancy and in premises associated with businesses.

A commonly-used Census indicator of income is levels is the degree of car ownership. Households without access to a motor vehicle are likely to be relatively deprived (though levels of car ownership are usually lower in cities than rural areas, due to the availability of good public transport). This indicator reveals a marked differential between white and minority ethnic groups in access to motor vehicles, with more than two-fifths of people from minority ethnic groups living in households with no car. However, this masks the even greater contrasts between minority ethnic groups. Two-thirds of Bangladeshi people and a slightly smaller percentage of Black-Other people lived in households with no car. At the other extreme, only a fifth of Indian people lived in a household without a car, and Chinese and Other-Asian people also displayed a higher rate of car ownership than white people. Black people and people from the Other-Other and Bangladeshi ethnic groups were most disadvantaged on this measure, with Pakistani people slightly more likely to live in households with cars.

Neighbourhood Deprivation

Variations in the degree of deprivation experienced by individual ethnic groups within an individual city are difficult to assess, because no data set exists on the income of ethnic groups in small areas. However, indicators of relative wealth in small areas can be derived from the Census, such as the percentage of households in overcrowded housing or the percentage without access to a private car. The relative deprivation of individual ethnic groups can then be compared by comparing that of the areas in which people from different ethnic groups live.

The Department of the Environment, Transport and the Regions has developed an 'Index of Local Disadvantage' using 1991 Census data for Enumeration Districts (which may be thought of as local neighbourhoods, each of which contains 200 households on average). The scores on this index are zero for areas which are less deprived than the average for all neighbourhoods in England, and is larger the greater the degree of deprivation. Here, the index value was used to classify Enumeration Districts in Birmingham into three groups; not deprived, less deprived and more deprived. The population of each ethnic group living in each of these three classes was summed, and expressed as a percentage of the total population of the ethnic group in the city (Table 9).

Table 9   Percentage of population living in neighbourhoods classified by degree of deprivation, 1991

Ethnic group	Population, 1991	Not deprived	Moderately deprived	Most deprived
White	749,061	23.5	60.7	15.8
Minority ethnic groups	*205,697*	*5.2*	*40.1*	*54.7*
Black	*55,936*	*4.4*	*47.9*	*47.7*
Black-Caribbean	44,503	4.2	47.4	48.3
Black-African	2,649	7.3	49.1	43.6
Black-Other	8,784	4.6	49.8	45.6
South Asian	*129,568*	*4.6*	*35.9*	*59.4*
Indian	50,877	9.5	55.8	34.7
Pakistani	65,967	1.6	24.7	73.7
Bangladeshi	12,724	0.8	15.0	84.2
Chinese and other	*20,193*	*10.9*	*45.5*	*43.5*
Chinese	3,152	20.8	48.4	30.7
Other-Asian	5,587	10.0	40.6	49.4
Other-Other	11,454	8.6	47.2	44.2
All ethnic groups	**954,758**	**19.6**	**56.3**	**24.2**
Born in Ireland	37,939	13.3	60.5	26.1

Overall, a fifth of Birmingham's population live in neighbourhoods which are classified as not deprived, and hence four-fifths live in 'moderately deprived' or 'most deprived' enumeration districts. However, there is great variation between ethnic groups in the chance of living in a deprived area. Nearly a quarter of white people live in environments classified as 'not deprived', compared with only one in 20 people from minority ethnic groups. Only one in six white people live in the 'most deprived' areas, compared with over half the minority population. Not all ethnic groups are equally deprived. A fifth of Chinese people and a tenth of Indian and Other-Asian people live in areas which are 'not deprived', though a third of Indian and a half of Other-Asian people live in the 'most deprived' neighbourhoods.

Black, Pakistani and Bangladeshi people are clearly more likely to live in deprived areas. Under 5 per cent of Black people live in 'not deprived' areas, but nearly half live in the 'most deprived' areas. Pakistani and Bangladeshi people are even more likely to be deprived, with nearly three-quarters of

Pakistani and 84.2 per cent of Bangladeshi people living in the 'most deprived' enumeration districts. The greater degree of deprivation of Black, Pakistani and Bangladeshi people is summarised in Figure 6, which presents mean neighbourhood deprivation scores by ethnic group. Other-Asian and Other-Other have similar neighbourhood deprivation scores to the three Black ethnic groups, but Chinese and Indian people again emerge as being less likely than people from other minority ethnic groups to live in deprived areas.

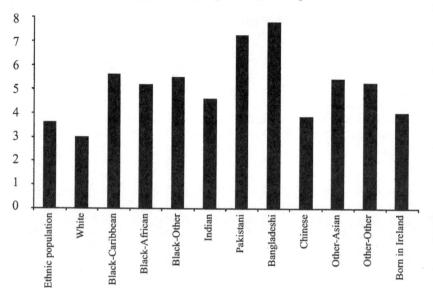

Figure 6   Mean neighbourhood deprivation score by ethnic group, 1991

These deprivation measures are clearly related to the degree of residential segregation between ethnic groups in Birmingham, with white people more likely to live in the more prosperous suburbs, and people from minority ethnic groups more likely to live in the relatively deprived inner areas of the city. This can be measured using the Index of Dissimilarity, which represents the percentage of the population from one ethnic group which would have to move for its spatial distribution to match that of another ethnic group (Table 10). The high degree of segregation which exists between white people and people from minority ethnic groups is demonstrated by the finding that nearly two-thirds of the latter would have to move for the geographical distribution of the two groups to become equal. People born in Ireland displayed a spatial distribution much more similar to that of white people as a whole. South

Asian people were more segregated than Black people. However, there was almost as much segregation between Black and South Asian people as there was between Black and white people, and substantial dissimilarity between the geographical distribution of Chinese and Other people and the two other broad minority ethnic groups.

Table 10   Segregation between broad ethnic groups, 1991: index of dissimilarity

Broad ethnic group	White	Born in Ireland	*Minority ethnic groups*	Black	South Asian	Chinese and other
White	–	25.4	*62.4*	54.1	72.3	50.2
Minority ethnic groups	62.4	50.0	–	33.0	16.8	33.1
Black	54.1	43.3	*33.0*	–	49.0	39.0
South Asian	72.3	61.7	*16.8*	49.0	–	44.7
Chinese and other	50.2	42.6	*33.1*	39.0	44.7	–
Born in Ireland	25.4	0.0	*50.0*	43.3	61.7	42.6

Table 11 demonstrates that the degree of segregation of individual ethnic groups was even greater. Bangladeshi people were most the segregated, displaying indices of dissimilarity of over 60 per cent when their residential distribution was compared with that of all other ethnic groups except Pakistani people. White people were more likely to live in the same areas as Black-Caribbean and Black-Other people than they were to live near people from other minority ethnic groups. The geographical distribution of Indian people was more similar to that of Black-Caribbean people than other South Asian people.

Crime

People from minority ethnic groups tend to be more likely than white people to be the victims of crime. One factor underlying this differential is that they tend to live in more deprived areas, in which crime is most common. However, they also tend to be more likely than white people to be charged with crimes, because crime is most common among the young and minority ethnic groups contain a high percentage of young people. Police statistics reveal that in 1993, 61.3 per cent of first time offenders in Birmingham were white, 14.6 per cent Black and 19.9 per cent Asian. Just over half of Black offenders (53.9 per cent) were first-time offenders, compared with 62 per cent of white

Table 11   Segregation between individual ethnic groups, 1991: index of dissimilarity

Ethnic group	White	Black -Caribbean	Black -African	Black -Other	Indian	Pakistani	Bangla- deshi	Chinese	Other Asian	Other- other	Born in Ireland
White	–	56.7	71.8	53.4	66.8	80.4	87.2	70.3	70.7	50.4	25.4
Black-Caribbean	56.7	–	57.1	33.6	49.4	63.3	66.1	67.8	57.0	43.6	45.7
Black-African	71.8	57.1	–	59.9	66.4	72.1	74.8	69.8	65.2	61.5	65.6
Black-Other	53.4	33.6	59.9	–	60.8	67.5	70.9	70.5	63.5	46.5	45.6
Indian	66.8	49.4	66.4	60.8	–	62.9	70.0	70.8	55.3	59.0	59.3
Pakistani	80.4	63.3	72.1	67.5	62.9	–	50.8	78.9	56.8	57.5	70.2
Bangladeshi	87.2	66.1	74.8	70.9	70.0	50.8	–	81.9	64.6	67.1	78.8
Chinese	70.3	67.8	69.8	70.5	70.8	78.9	81.9	–	67.6	67.5	68.2
Other Asian	70.7	57.0	65.2	63.5	55.3	56.8	64.6	67.6	v	56.6	64.0
Other-Other	50.4	43.6	61.5	46.5	59.0	57.5	67.1	67.5	56.6	–	44.0
Born in Ireland	25.4	45.7	65.6	45.6	59.3	70.2	78.8	68.2	64.0	44.0	–

and 70.5 per cent of Asian offenders. The peak age group for offending was 15 year olds in 1993, more than 5 per cent of whom had committed an offence. Rates of crime were highest in the City centre/Ladywood (in which 7.2 per cent of all young people had committed offences), Nechells/Duddeston (6 per cent) and Winson Green/Hockley (5.2 per cent). The lowest rates of youth offending occurred in Moseley/Billesley (1.4 per cent), Yardley/South Yardley (1.7 per cent) and Sparkbrook/Sparkhill/Tyseley (1.7 per cent). More than half (53.5 per cent) of youth offenders were school children, with a further 22.5 per cent unemployed; only 5.3 per cent were in work. The most common offences were theft from retail premises (21.4 per cent).[2] By 1998, the peak age for offending was 16 (781 offenders – nearly 6 per cent of the age group), and 59 per cent of all youth offenders were white, 20 per cent Afro-Caribbean and 14 per cent Asian. Of the 2142 young people sentenced, 52 per cent were white, 17 per cent Afro-Caribbean and 7 per cent Asian.[3] The percentage of young people committing crime was higher in the eastern wards of the city than in the western and central wards, in which the minority share of the population was highest.

In the late 1990s, the Birmingham Partnership Against Racial Harassment (BPARH) recorded 480 incidents in a single year, more than a third of which were car or property damage, twice as large as the second identified category, verbal abuse (17 per cent), with a further 12 per cent of incidents involving physical violence, 6 per cent written racist material and a further 5 per cent graffiti.[4] A fifth were classified as 'Other' (which includes a small number of incidents of arson). These figures are certainly an underestimate, and the number of racial incidents recorded in police statistics was 1,548 during 1999/2000.

The use of 'stop and search' powers by the police clearly has a much greater impact on Black people (especially in the 17–20 age group) than on people from other ethnic groups (Figure 7). The police have been making less use of 'stop and search' powers in the last few years and are attempting to use their powers in a more focused manner. The number of searches conducted by West Midlands Police declined by 19 per cent between 1998/99 and 1999/2000 to 20,341, with little change in the ethnic mix. The evidence seems to confirm that 'stop and search' powers were being used in a more 'targeted' fashion, since the number of arrests as a result of searches increased by 9.9 per cent for Black suspects and 28.8 per cent for Asian suspects (Figure 8). Of those searched 63 per cent were white, 15.4 per cent Black and 20.3 per cent Asian. However, the percentage of the population (estimated for 1998) experiencing stops and searches varied considerably by age and ethnic group. In Birmingham, stops and searches represented only 0.6 per cent of the white

population, but 1.6 per cent of the Asian and 3.1 per cent of the Black population.[5] The peak age group for stops and searches was 17 to 20 year olds, 3,462 stops and searches, representing 6.1 in every 100 people. However, this ratio was 7.1 for Asian people and 16.5 for Black young people.

There was a similar differential in the ratio of the number of arrests to the population by age and ethnic group, with a further marked contrast by gender (Figures 9 and 10). There were 8.1 arrests per 100 men, but only 1.3 arrests per 100 women, with arrest rates highest for 17 to 20 year olds at 32.8 per 100 men and 5.2 per 100 women. Arrest rates were highest for Black people; 20.4 per 100 men and 3.3 per 100 women, followed by Asian (4.8 per 100) and white people (4.1 per 100). Ethnic differentials were similar for men and women, except that Asian women (0.7 per 100) were much less likely than Asian men (8.6 per 100) to be arrested. The most disturbing feature of the data is that arrests of Black men aged 17 to 20 represented 81.3 per cent of the number of Black men in this age group.

The use of custodial sentences for young offenders has increased recently. In 1998, two-thirds (67 per cent) of those given custodial sentences were white, but 17 per cent were Afro-Caribbean, 6 per cent Asian and 3 per cent of 'mixed parentage'.[6]

Education and Schools

Of the 177,965 pupils in Birmingham schools during 1998/99, 59.3 per cent were white, 6.8 per cent Afro-Caribbean, 16.5 per cent Pakistani, 6.8 per cent Indian, 3.6 per cent Bangladeshi and 3.6 per cent of 'mixed' heritage. There was little difference in ethnic composition between the primary and secondary sectors taken as a whole, but there was clear evidence that white and Indian pupils were more likely than Pakistani pupils to have places in Grant Maintained schools. In the Grant Maintained sector, 83.9 per cent of primary pupils were white, while only 3.2 per cent Pakistani, and 67.6 per cent of secondary pupils were white (9.6 per cent Indian and 9.1 per cent Pakistani). There was little difference in the share of African-Caribbean pupils between different types of school.

Pupils with poorer achievement in education generally come from the African-Caribbean, Bangladeshi and Pakistani ethnic groups, together with white boys. Figures 11 to 13 demonstrate how educational achievements have improved during the second half of the 1990s for boys and girls from each ethnic group, compared with the average.

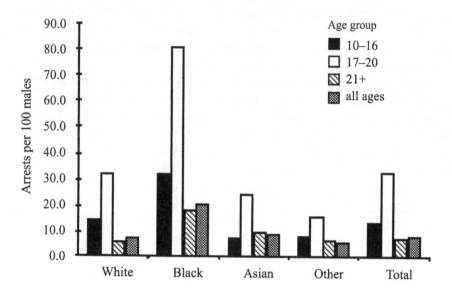

Figure 9   Arrests per 100 males, Birmingham, 1999/2000

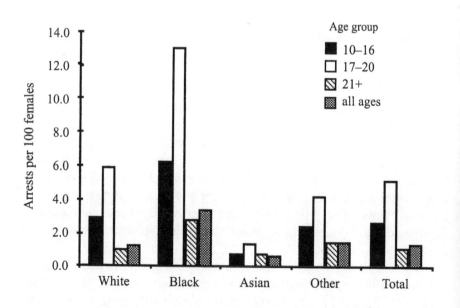

Figure 10   Arrests per 100 females, Birmingham, 1999/2000

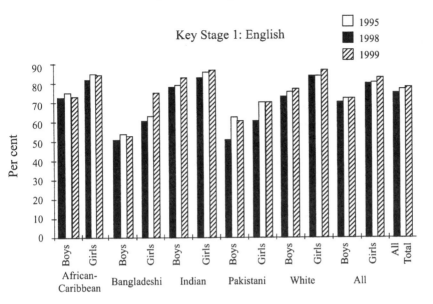

Figure 11   Trends in per cent achieving Key Stage 1 in English

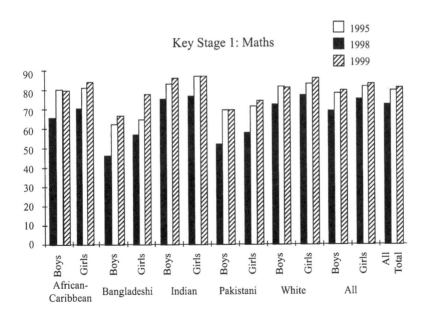

Figure 12   Trends in per cent achieving Key Stage 1 in Maths

Figures 11 and 12 compare the percentages achieving Key Stage 1 in Mathematics and English over the period from 1995 to 1999. At Key Stage 1, the gender differential is present in every ethnic group, with girls doing better than boys. This differential seems to be wider in English than in Maths. White, Indian and African-Caribbean girls perform best in English, but Indian girls and boys seem to perform best in mathematics, followed by girls and boys from the white and African-Caribbean ethnic groups. Improvements in performance through the 1990s were greater in Mathematics than in English, with differentials in achievement between the most successful and least successful (Bangladeshi boys) sections of the school population widening.

By the end of the period of compulsory schooling, differentials in achievement have widened. The gender differential in achievement was maintained, with girls being substantially more likely than boys to attain five or more GCSEs at A* to C level in 1998/99 (Figure 13), girls performine better than boys in each ethnic group. Indian girls displayed the highest level of achievement, followed by white girls, Indian boys and Bangladeshi girls. The least successful group by a wide margin was African-Caribbean boys, though Bangladeshi and Pakistani boys also performed poorly. Among girls, African-Caribbean and Pakistani girls were least likely to obtain five or more A* to C grades in their GCSEs. Girls' achievement improved faster than that

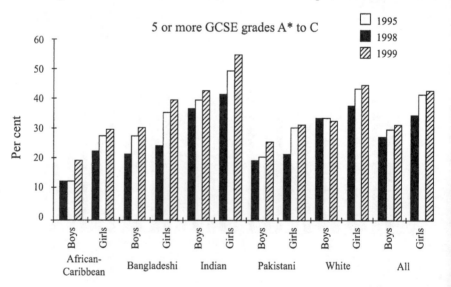

Figure 13   Percentage of pupils achieving 5 or more GCSEs at grade A* to C, 1998/9

of boys during the period 1995 to 1999, particularly for Bangladeshi and Pakistani girls. White and Indian boys improved their performance more slowly than boys from other ethnic groups over this period. Though African-Caribbean boys displayed the poorest performance throughout this period, there was evidence of marked improvement in performance between 1997/98 and 1998/99.

Another indicator of underachievement in education is the permanent exclusion of pupils by schools, on the grounds of their violent behaviour or their causing major disruption to teaching and learning in the school.[7] During 1998/99, in the West Midlands (former) metropolitan county as a whole, 3.6 per cent of secondary schools fell in the 100 schools with the highest incidence of permanent exclusions in England (against 2.8 per cent for England as a whole and 6.3 per cent for Outer London). In Birmingham, 338 pupils were permanently excluded from Birmingham schools during the academic year 1998/99, 55.6 per cent of whom were white, 13.9 per cent Asian and 18.3 per cent Afro-Caribbean. The Afro-Caribbean share of exclusions had fallen from its peak of 34.8 per cent during 1994/95 (when there were 348 exclusions in total), while the share of white and mixed parentage pupils in the number of exclusions had increased over the same period. The great majority (84.3 per cent) of those excluded were boys, while 63.8 per cent of excluded Asians were of Pakistani ethnic origin. In England as a whole, 0.59 per cent of Black-Caribbean pupils were excluded during 1998/99, compared with an average for all ethnic groups of 0.17 per cent, 0.1 per cent of Pakistani pupils and 0.04 per cent of Indian pupils (DfEE, 2000). In Birmingham, the number of excluded African-Caribbean pupils was 0.48 per cent of the (estimated 1998) population aged 0–15, compared with 0.18 per cent for white pupils and 0.13 per cent for Asian pupils.

Conclusion

This chapter has brought together information from a range of sources, in order to provide a picture of the living conditions of minority ethnic groups in Birmingham in the 1990s. Clearly, the city's minority population is substantial and has continued to grow rapidly, now forming the majority in some parts of the city and some age groups. The services provided by the city such as education and social services can no longer ignore the considerable ethnic diversity of the population, and face the twin challenges of making the delivery of services sensitive to different cultural needs, and ensuring that these services offer equal opportunities for employment and career advancement to all ethnic groups. Moreover, the city's employers have had to recognise the economically wasteful nature of racially discriminatory recruitment and employment policies in the face of an increasing share of young people entering the labour market being from minority ethnic groups, while entrepreneurs have been presented with new market opportunities in serving a population of increasing ethnic diversity.

However, there are marked geographical variations in ethnic composition and levels of prosperity within the city. Minority ethnic groups tend to be concentrated into the central parts of the city, in which unemployment rates are higher, housing conditions are poorer and levels of income lower. Segregation statistics reveal that individual ethnic groups tend to cluster together, rather than live in general 'minority' areas. Overall, people from minority ethnic groups are disadvantaged relative to white people, but there is a gradation of disadvantage, with Indians and Chinese least disadvantaged, Pakistani and Bangladeshi people most disadvantaged, and Black people somewhere between the two. People from the Indian and Pakistani ethnic groups are more likely than Black people to own their own homes, and thus many are constrained by the housing market to live in areas of cheaper housing. Even in the social rented sector (most important for Black and Bangladeshi people) there is an issue of people from minority ethnic groups having poorer opportunities than white people to move to the outer areas of Birmingham.

Other indicators also emphasise the disadvantage and 'social exclusion' faced by some ethnic groups. For example, people from all minority ethnic groups experience higher unemployment rates than white people, and have lower levels of activity in the labour market. However, there is evidence of economic progress by some minority ethnic groups, such as Indian and Chinese people, who now display the highest levels of educational attainment in the city. On the other hand, African-Caribbean people still suffer from the poorest educational performance, and are most at risk of being 'stopped and searched' or arrested by the police. This ethnic group, and others marginalised by language and poverty (e.g. Bangladeshis and people from less numerous ethnic groups who have arrived recently as asylum seekers), thus face the prospect of continued disadvantage.

Acknowledgements

This chapter draws heavily upon data from the 1991 Census of Population.

This data is Crown Copyright, but was made available for use by the academic sector through a joint ESRC/JISC purchase.

Notes

1 A phrase used to describe the expected fall in the number of young people at the end of the twentieth century which was identified by British planners and policy makers in the late 1980s.
2 West Midlands Police (1994) Youth Offender Profile: Birmingham 1993.
3 West Midlands Joint Data Team (1999) Youth Offender Profile Birmingham 1998.
4 Birmingham Community Safety Partnership (1999) Birmingham's Crime and Disorder Audit.
5 Though a recent Home Office study has suggested that these type of statistics may be inappropriate, since the denominator is the resident population of the area. A more appropriate denominator is the daytime population (people working, studying and shopping in the city centre), of which people from minority ethnic groups form a larger share of the total in most cities (Miller, 2000).
6 Birmingham City Council Social Services Department (1999) Youth Justice Annual Report 1998.
7 Schools with high permanent exclusion rates tend to have low levels of pupil attainment and high percentages of pupils eligible for free school meals (DfEE, 2000).

Chapter Five

Blacks in British Society: Categorisation and Ethnicity

Introduction

British society and its population of immigrant origin are often conceptualised in terms of ethnic communities. A number of factors have contributed to the formation of ethnic communities including the spatial distribution related to the structure of housing which led to the geographical concentration of minorities, the character of the chain migration and the political management of those populations, particularly at local level. Indeed, not only have municipalities made a space for the recognition of ethnic communities but they have also encouraged their consolidation through the search for gatekeepers and representatives among those groups. Ethnicity thus has become embedded in institutional practices as it constitutes a basis upon which resources are allocated (Candappa and Joly 1994). Those populations are also the target of racism and racist discrimination, prevalent despite the legislation introduced to combat it. This chapter examines how the young people in the group under study position themselves and navigate within this context.

Birmingham and its Ethnic Minorities

Birmingham is the second city in Britain with a population of about two million within the geographical limits of the municipality. Moreover, the city is part of a large industrial conurbation, the West Midlands, without any break in the industrial and urban landscape of the towns and cities which compose the region: Sandwell, Wolverhampton, Dudley, Walsall, West Bromwich, Solihull and Coventry.

Birmingham is an industrial city which, at the beginning of the Industrial Revolution was named the Workshop of Great Britain, and known as such by de Tocqueville and Dickens (quoted by Chinn 1994), and which also became an important commercial centre. Among a great diversity of trades, small metal work, motor industry, cycle industry, light armaments and jewellery have contributed to the prosperity of Birmingham which even the crisis of the 1930s left undented. In industry, nonferrous metals, aeroplane engines, machine tools and electrical machines have made part of the industrial landscape. Traditionally Birmingham is a place where class conflicts are characterised by moderation and by the political cooperation between workers and employers (Chinn 1994). The Labour majority on the council since 1981 is moderate, middle of the road. Demands made by its population are moderate and even among its residents of foreign origin (of whom Muslims are the most numerous), political participation is integrated on the whole within the political structures of the society of reception. This corresponds to a general tendency where Asians are concerned in Britain. Thus, as a whole the history of Birmingham has not been notable for its violence and yet, Birmingham was shaken by so-called race riots in 1981 and 1985, at the same time as a number of large British cities including Manchester and London.

In the 1980s, recession brought about the closure of numerous factories and 107,205 jobs were lost between 1978 and 1989 (Chinn 1994), in the wake of the decline of the steel and motor industry. The 2 per cent rate of unemployment in 1966 reached 21 per cent in 1981. Most disadvantaged areas have been even more affected, for instance, 30.1 per cent at the end of the 1980s in the Small Heath constituency (Chinn 1994). Taking into account also the precariousness of employment and the lowering of wages, this means that the average income has gone down considerably. This process coincided with the generalised reduction of public services and an accelerated privatisation of sectors which were previously managed by the municipality from state funding. The Conservative government of 1979 established monetarist policy *à la* Milton Friedman and an ideology where individualism reigned followed the defeat of the National Union of Mineworkers (NUM) in 1987 and caused the destruction of numerous local communities. Shortly before she resigned, indeed, Margaret Thatcher announced that there was no such thing as 'society'. For more than a decade, the Welfare State has been under threat. Today Great Britain is in the throes of a crisis of an economic, social, political and ideological nature; Birmingham is no exception.

The strata which are most affected by these events are social strata which are the most disadvantaged and among which unemployment is severe: on the one hand, is the outer ring of the city, which means white working class areas, and on the other hand is the inner city with its strong population of ethnic minority background. Young people are affected by the crisis more than anyone. Birmingham is a multicultural city which received successive arrivals of immigrants and refugees of Caribbean, Bangladeshi, Chilean, Chinese,

Indian, Irish, Italian, Jewish, Pakistani, Vietnamese and Yemeni origin. All these groups today form communities which are settled and whose children have grown up in Britain and are British. They have created a network of associations with varied functions many of which negotiate with the municipality, (Joly 1995; Candappa and Joly 1994).

During the last 15 years, several studies have been carried out on the populations of ethnic minority background in Birmingham. This permits an appreciation of social interaction among those groups and leads us to focus the present research on young Blacks whose parents came from Caribbean islands after the Second World War.

People of Asian origin from the Indian peninsula, on the whole, have constituted dense communities with networks and numerous associations covering economic, political, social, cultural and religious domains, accompanied by an ethnic mobilisation and a political participation which are both very strong, mainly among the ranks of the Labour Party and at the local level of the municipality. This has been largely documented and the apparent success of these groups (except for Bangladeshis) provide young Asians with identity and community resources which seem to enable them to access participation to the majority society without a manifest crisis, thanks to the collective project which the group carries but which also allows a space for individual projects. To an extent they have thus been protected against the effects of economic neo-liberalism established by the Conservative government from 1979 to 1997. Another characteristic of this group resides in the limited amount of violent acts which emanate from it although they themselves are victims of racist violence.

The working-class of autochthonous origin which occupies social housing in the outer-ring social estates was severely hit by the recession and neo-liberal economic policy through unemployment and the precariousness of jobs which it brought about. In addition, other social and ideological factors have constructed a difficult situation for young people, characterised by problems in group identification and by the lack of objective and aspirations for their future although they have managed to follow idiosyncratic processes of group identification such as football team allegiances. Delinquency, pub brawls, racist aggression and hooliganism are the acts of violence which are most common among those groups.

The young African-Caribbeans are always signalled by the media and the common notion as the most problematic ones. They are associated with violence, either individual, in the shape of mugging and delinquency or collective, in the shape of riots as in 1981 and 1985. They are severely hit by unemployment and are victims of strong discrimination where association and community networks are less manifest among these groups than among Asians.

It is probable that the relationship to violence among these diverse populations, and the shape and the meaning of this violence are differentiated as a function of the populations studied. We have decided to select young African-Caribbeans for a more detailed study.

Sociological Intervention

The data gathered on the young African-Caribbeans was obtained through sociological intervention. As a methodology sociological intervention derives from a specific theory of social action as developed by Alain Touraine (1973) within a Weberian framework: in his view social action is meaningful and subjectively oriented by responses to a situation because it is defined by social actors' commitment to values, principles and rules. Moreover, social action cannot be separated from the social relations within which it is produced. According to Touraine (1973) action is constructed through the integration of three principles:

- identity: how the actor defines himself;
- opposition: how the actor defines his opponent;
- totality: what is at stake in this relationship (Dubet 1999).

> Sociological intervention starts from the idea that the nature of a collective behaviour can be best known by interpreting the work performed by a group of actors as it analyses its own actions under conditions created by researchers and managed by both parties. (Touraine 1978, p. 296)

The collective action being researched is studied through bringing together a group of actors, about 12 persons, on a regular basis together with researchers and 'interlocutors' (protagonists). This method presupposes that actors can know what they are doing and see through ideologies and the spontaneous categories of practices (Dubet and Wieviorka 1996). It is based on the notion that a debate between actors and researchers within set conditions can produce knowledge. It works on what is said, the group's history and the analyses worked out during discussions. As the study progresses, the researcher proposes an interpretation of the collective action based on a hypothesis.

During some of the sessions, interlocutors who are significant others in the life of the actors and their social relations are invited to debate with the group: they may be allies or opponents of the collective action. A kind of laboratory condition of the social action is thus created. Those 'open' sessions are interspersed with closed sessions wherein the group and the researchers make an analysis of previous encounters, with the aim of arriving at an increasingly analytical attitude. The interlocutors place the actors in a social relationship. The confrontation between the group and the interlocutors may bring out contradictions among members of the group and between rationalised discourse and practice. The variations observed reveal issues which ideology may cover up. As a final result, the research aims to produce knowledge and increase the actors' capacity for action.

In this study the sociological intervention group includes young Blacks whose parents are of Afro-Caribbean origin, except for one young woman who comes from a mixed parentage (an Afro-Caribbean mother and an Irish father), and a young man who was adopted by white parents. All except two are of modest social background. They live in a variety of districts of the city, some of which have a strong ethnic minority population and others not. Several are students, some work and others are unemployed. The group comprises seven young men and four young women, the youngest is 17 and the eldest 27. They are single except for one young man who is living now with his second partner and his daughters. Among the others, six live with their parents or their mother while four live on their own or share accommodation with friends. They live in diversified areas of Birmingham: five different areas of the inner city, three white working class areas and one area populated by students and intellectuals. Two of them work as community workers or youth workers in community centres, three are studying at university, two are preparing for 'A' Levels; one receives a permanent sickness allowance and the last one is unemployed. Some of the students also work part-time to fund their studies. Several of them belong to groups and associations such as church, musical group, a European radio, the Sickle Cell Anaemia Association; all have varied interests which articulate mainly around music and culture. The interlocutors included a Black theologian, an engineering trade-union representative, a Residents Association representative, the leader of the City Council, a Pan-Africanist community leader, representatives from large British companies, a police superintendent, a Black stand-up comedian, and a Black policewoman. It proved difficult to obtain the participation of a representative from the Department of Health and Social Security, a delegate from a teaching trade union and a media person. The study spread over 14 sessions of two hours each which were entirely tape-recorded and transcribed. Two researchers and one research secretary took part in each session.

Categorisation and Racism

The young African-Caribbeans have been categorised by white majority society on race/colour lines. One main characteristic of the Black condition is well documented in Anglo-Saxon literature (UK and US): the question of racism and racist discrimination. A variety of analyses and explanations have been advanced to account for these but what remains is the continuous experience of racism described by the young people in the group. It covers the minutiae of everyday social interaction but also their interfacing with all the major institutions of the majority society. To quote the CRE's submission to Lord Scarman's inquiry into the Brixton disorders, 'the Black community face a level of prejudice and discrimination not within the experience of any other group in this country' (CRE 1981, p. 10).

Racist Prejudice Every Day

The young African-Caribbeans in this sociological intervention group are first and foremost victims of a debilitating categorisation and a negative racialisation. What is hitting them is a pejorative ascription, concomitant with racist and discriminatory practices. The youths are confronted by this racism in a continuous manner, recurring without respite.

William: You face racism every day, you have to deal with it.

Daryl: We as Black people have always had a struggle, we live in a world where we are stereotyped.

Those who were brought up in areas other than those of the inner city experienced a virtual mental state of siege as they constantly had to be on their guard, ready to defend themselves, like this young woman who attended a white school:

Alice: I went to a Catholic school, it's like, no Black people, zero amount of Black people, so I had to defend myself then.

The stereotype is such that it occupies the British *imaginaire* and persists. For instance, the common image of the mugger is that of a young Black, regardless of statistical evidence.

> Donald: For one example, stereotypes. Black people are, as said by Paul Condon, that we are all muggers.

The stereotype is so widespread that practically anybody residing in England would be able to define its main characteristics peddled by the media: Black people are 'excessively exuberant', 'noisy', 'undisciplined', 'aggressive'. The young people in the group are acutely aware of this and quote it themselves.

> Donald: Asians are looked up differently to Blacks by the English. They're seen as civilised and we're still seen as loose cannons, unorganised. Asian people are more focused and seen as more similar to the English than the Blacks.

Physical violence and aggression are also perceived as their attributes and several of the young people mentioned it.

> Daryl: The negative things that are thought about you, are always put in your face before you can make a move. Like why are Black people so often associated with violence.

> William: Black people are seen as aggressive, and it's misinterpreted, you know.

If they fight against racist harassment, they are said to have a chip on their shoulder, which again confirms the stereotype.

> Ian: And if you try to retaliate, you're a typical Black person, always opening up their mouths.

As a consequence they feel that they cannot behave in a natural manner but must modify their way of being in order to protect themselves against prejudice. They have to conform to the norms of behaviour and attitudes acceptable to the majority white society.

> Donald: And in this country, if you behave that way you find yourself being picked up all of the time, so you have to tone it down, dilute it and act Eurocentric, the way white people want you to act, otherwise you're seen as aggressive.

Moreover, public opinion and the media tend to consider that young African-Caribbeans are all involved in delinquency or drug trafficking.

Another characteristic attributed to them goes very far back in the colonial imagination and the slave trade, in the shape of an assumed overdeveloped sexuality which pertains to abnormality. As one of the young people explained, this is linked to an attempt to dehumanise them. According to those young people, such notions still seem to influence the behaviour of some elements of the majority society.

> Donald: Well, back in the day when the first explorers came to Africa and were studying the natives, they wrote about African people, and to dehumanise Black people, they wrote about Black people in a certain way, to say that their genitalia was of a larger size, the shape of a donkey and stuff, about their buttocks and those kinds of things. I mean, how many times have you stood at the urinal in the toilet and there's always someone turning round.

The media reflect this imagery as illustrated by an advertisement on television which one of them quotes.

> Alice: What he wanted to tell us by showing us this was that people in society, no matter how high up the ladder (cos this guy was wearing a three piece suit), a Black man is always defined by his sexuality because of the size etc.

What is more sinister is that stereotypes and prejudices inevitably bring about negative attitudes or hostile behaviour from the majority society. Whether they be individuals such as shopkeepers.

> Daryl: So I walk in the shop in Handsworth and I go down the aisle. The man hums and stands near to me. But next time I'll confront him and say 'listen, not all Black people are thieves'. It's that same stigma.

or institutions like the police:

> Donald: Also a lot of white police officers don't come from multiracial areas so they're not really around Black people unless there's an incident say at a party or a club. They don't really mix with Black people, so their perception of a Black person is from the TV or reading the newspaper. The way Black people are portrayed on the TV is like making moves, you know, he must be doing something, he's got a portable phone, the fast car, he's short-tempered and will fight over

anything. All these things, they're very physical, loud mouthed, all these things go through a white person's head. And you know when they take a Black person down, I mean arrest them? They're usually more physical than if it was say a white person, just because they think that this person could do them some harm, so they go in rough all the time. It's just stereotypes.

This situation is encountered every day without ever disappearing and even though it is more pronounced for young men, young women also suffer from it. The young people of the group quote many examples to demonstrate it. The most telling one is that of Alice, who when she had plaits which made it possible to identify her as African-Caribbean, was treated 'accordingly'. Now that she wears a scarf because she converted to Islam she notices that shopkeepers do not follow her around as soon as she enters a shop.

> Alice: No, because before I became a Muslim, I dressed like a regular Black girl. You might walk into a shop and find three white women following you waiting for you steal. They think automatically that you will steal, and they ask to look in your bag as a 'routine check'.

The positive characteristics quoted for Black people are principally their quality as good sportsmen or women, musicians and dancers, but not intellectual qualities. This is corroborated by their experience at school, examined below.

All this is constructed as the norm for African-Caribbeans in contrast with white English people, who are deemed to be very different, apart from eccentrics or deviants; mentioned here are only some of the negative attributes imposed on them by the majority society. Their entire life is dominated by those stigmas. The young people note that they cannot escape from this prejudice and that individual qualities do not count. They are very clear about the mechanisms which categorise them as such and the necessity to combat those without falling into violence. Violence is not one of the options envisaged. They are conscious of obstacles which interfere between their aspirations and realising them, as a consequence of racism and discrimination. They also come up against a wall of incomprehension even from white people who are their friends because this experience of racism cannot possibly be imagined.

> Donald: But white people on the whole live in a different reality to Black people. You can sit down with your white friends and tell them what happened to you, like you went into a bus stop, and some old woman, you know the look, we all know the look. There's a certain look you get, and you know it without them even saying a word. You know

the look. The bag comes closer to them and you think, shut up, I've got loads a money. You don't say that, but that's what you're thinking. You explain that to a white person and they say 'well, may be you was, blah, blah because of this', and ... they live in a different reality.

School

Education and schools are one of the most recurrent themes in the young people's discourse. School obviously represents an important stake for them, as a potential instrument of social mobility, but in practice it is a missed opportunity resulting from prejudice. They also perceive it as a possible vehicle for ethnic and cultural awareness, carriers of dignity and self-worth, if educational structures allow for it.

Interaction with institutions begins with school and in the young people's opinion, with it prejudice also starts. School underachievement is a common feature among young African-Caribbeans and so is conflict within the school. Black children are up to 15 times more likely to be excluded from schools in some areas than their white classmates (Equalities Division Bulletin January 1999). Teachers tend to consider young African-Caribbean's as difficult elements who disrupt the class, and at best encourage them to pursue sport or music. Sport and music, which in other contexts can be celebrated and glorified because of Black people's outstanding successes in those domains, are perceived here as a stigma. They are little valued in the education system, and young Blacks are pigeonholed into them to the exclusion of 'academic' subjects which require 'brain' rather than muscles or emotions.

> Ian: When you're at school they push you to do typical Black people things like sport and music.

This is a most frequent occurrence mentioned by all the young people in our group. Moreover, they generally attended schools in rather deprived areas and where it is difficult to do very well. Even in a school which had the reputation of being a 'good' school before the arrival of African-Caribbean pupils, young Blacks had the impression that teachers became uninterested in their school achievements.

> Sandra: I went to a mostly Black populated school, in a white area. It was known to be a good school. But when the Black people started going there, it was like the teachers didn't care. They didn't encourage us to go into good professional jobs, they encouraged us to be singers.

According to the young people in the group, their self-confidence is undermined by the British school system.

> Daryl: But there's something about the British education system that saps the confidence of Black students, it takes your confidence away.

One of the young people blames in part the Eurocentric curriculum which marginalises and inferiorises Black people.

> Larry: But when I was taught history, it wasn't about Martin Luther King, I was taught white history all the way.

School underachievement among African-Caribbeans is so well recognised that it motivated an official enquiry at the initiative of a government body, the Rampton Report and numerous conclusive studies (Coard 1971; Troyna 1987). African-Caribbean's are also over-represented among long-term or permanent exclusions from school. It is almost possible to demonstrate that they are categorised as bad pupils not only by the label that they are given but also in its consequences, since young African-Caribbeans who appeared to perform well in the first few years of primary school, become the worst at the end of compulsory schooling. Those who make good are rare, particularly where boys are concerned. To be selected and given access to some courses is an achievement in itself. Ian signals that he is the only African-Caribbean in his *haute couture* course.

> Ian: So many Black people are leaving school, and failing to do well in or out of school. Look how many minority ethnic people applied for my course, I'm one in 10 people and I just about got accepted, they didn't want me on there. They hold the power! I'm one of the only Black people out of 80 students in the fashion industry, how many Black people does the fashion industry employ?

Employment

Employment is often linked to qualifications. One can thus expect that the young people concerned would be handicapped from the start because of underachievement at school. But this handicap is accentuated and even surpassed by discriminatory practices, whether they be institutional or individual (Wrench 1996).

Miriam: They look at the qualifications, and they might be the same, but the white man gets the job.

How many times have young people been rejected after obtaining an interview on the basis of a CV or a telephone call. It is impossible to identify them as Black by their name or even their accent, since most of them have acquired the accent of the area where they were brought up in Britain. However when they appear for the interview, they are told 'Sorry, the post is gone.' There seems to be an equation between African-Caribbean and menial employment. One of the young women describes the astonishment of customers in the restaurant where she works as a waitress during the summer, when she tells them that she is a university student.

Daryl: They look at your skin colour and they see you in a waitress uniform and they expect you to speak with a deep southern American accent, 'Yes boss, you want wibs wid dat boss!' They expect you to be really stupid.

The young people notice that they have to be twice as qualified and more competent and hard-working than their white peers to arrive at the same result.

Simon: It's true. I work in Marks and Spencers, and I think I'm the second Black person out of 200 staff. You always feel like you have to make that extra effort, like yes sir! Please sir!

Donald: You have to prove yourself three times as much as the next man.

They also note the infinitely small proportion of African-Caribbeans who occupy important posts or hold a profession.

Donald: There is also the glass ceiling effect, whereby even if you're good at your job, there's only a certain height you can go to.

Alice: I think that in this country and others, Black people aren't given opportunities. Those that they are given are only as far as what people want them to get, they're not going to get any higher.

Employment is their main preoccupation and most of the young people in the group are studying to increase their chances of success as they are so conscious of the difficulties ahead.

Health

The British health system has introduced two classes of treatment: patients who can afford it and take out a private insurance and those who have to rely on the National Health Service. However, discrimination in health was not tackled in our group along those lines. It was broached through the question of sickle cell anaemia because Sally, one of the members of the group, is severely affected: she is permanently exhausted has problems walking and needs crutches, and she suffers pain in her joints. In addition she needs to be hospitalised one or two weeks a month for a blood transfusion. During all her schooling she kept missing school and was never in a position to catch up. Schooling in the hospital was lacking, so she has no qualifications. If she looks for a job she cannot keep it because she is absent too often. The young people are conscious of the discriminatory dimension of this illness as it affects populations whose origins are in tropical regions where malaria reigns. In Britain this means mostly African-Caribbeans. However, the government has refused to grant this illness a specific status on a par with others like multiple sclerosis, which would permit those who are affected to benefit from supplementary resources and support.

> Sally: The money donated to Sickle Cell is not much. I went on TV to say that the disease should be listed as a dangerous disease, because it is, but they said it isn't killing a lot or enough people, So why should it be listed as dangerous? If it's not giving them pain, then they don't care. I'm in pain every day of my life. I just think that more money should be spent on Black concerning issues. Maybe then we would get some.

One even more worrying area is that of mental health. One of the young women mentioned the astonishment of her neighbours who saw her mother burning feathers on the chicken before cooking it. Their worried looks told a lot about what they thought of the mental state of the mother in question, or even their immediate association with voodoo practices. This is only an anecdote, but on a more serious plane, young African-Caribbean are disproportionately represented among diagnostics of schizophrenia.

> Daryl: You have unbelievable amounts in mental institutions. That comes from a lack of understanding, cos when you talk Patois, or put up your arms when you speak, cos that's the way you act, they think you're crazy.

The Police 'and Company'

The relationship between young African-Caribbeans and the police is antagonistic and racism in the police towards them is well known (Scarman Report 1981). Problems in this area are internal as well as external. This has unfortunately been confirmed yet again by the Stephen Lawrence enquiry (Macpherson 1999).

> Daryl: But the problems are out there and within the police structure. And the attitude towards young Black children needs to be dealt with as well.

One of the speakers to our group, a young African-Caribbean policewoman, gave a number of statistics supporting this statement. The police force is a white institution which finds it very difficult to integrate allogeneous elements.

> Police   Of that 7,800 officers only 200 are so-called ethnic minorities. Now,
> Officer: they recruit quite a few ethnic minorities as they put it, but unfortunately they have about a 90 per cent drop-out rate.

Young African-Caribbeans report being constantly confronted with stop and search harassment. They are the first ones to be suspected in the event of fights or some disorder.

> Daryl: On my way to work I get stopped by the police, they always question me on where I'm going etc. One time, I was surprised because they stopped and questioned me about a robbery. He asked me more questions and came back and was surprised that I didn't have a criminal record.

Young men are the main target but young women are also affected.

> Alice: Like my sister. She got arrested on a vague description, and she was kept in a cell overnight. She had no drinks. Then they let her out and said sorry, bye. But she just had a really traumatic experience and had done nothing wrong.

The animated debate which arises on this question in our group reveals that the shadow of the police is a fundamental element which structures the environment of young Black people.

Donald: A lot of the problems from my youth and still today, have a lot to do
            with the police.

Blacks are disproportionately represented among those who are arrested,
charged and taken to court. The police have completely adopted the stereotype
of young African-Caribbeans as delinquent, troublemakers and drug traffickers
as demonstrated by their practices. The young people are aware of their own
powerlessness. The proof of it, they say, is that one of them can be the victim
of police brutality without any recourse and that if African-Caribbeans die
during an arrest or in prison, no explanation is given and no condemnation
attributed.

Alice: Because a lot of people do complain about the brutality towards
            Black people.

Donald: The police scare me because whether you've done anything or not,
            if they want to push your face in, they can kill you and say it was
            misadventure or whatever. Throughout the years, a number of Black
            people have been arrested and gone missing. It just happens a lot
            with Black people, more than any other race of people. Like that
            woman who got deported, she had tape put round her head and face
            and mouth and she suffocated.

The young people also consider police impunity as a blatant proof of injustice:

Donald: But none of those police officers are being convicted of killing a
            Black person.

The judiciary system and the nature of its officers, i.e. judges, are perceived
to add to police practices to further tilt the balance against African-Caribbeans.
The young people signal that judges cumulate class prejudices and racist
prejudice against them.

Larry: If you get done for a burglary when you're 13, and you're walking
            down the street two weeks later and they've got a burglary to solve
            and they see you, you can get stitched up for it and you go to Solihull
            or Warwick crown court and you're finished. 'Well you're Black,
            unemployed and from Chelmsley Wood, we don't even want to look
            at anything else! This man is guilty!'

The young people in the group can testify to this through their own personal experience. Three of the fellows have been in jail and two of the girls mention that their father or brother were in jail; this does not include those who were cautioned. As far as these young people are concerned, prison makes part and parcel of their horizon as a natural element linked to the Black condition and does not cause surprise. Prison is almost a factor creating or consolidating social networks.

Alice: Another bad thing is you get to know everyone in the prison. It might sound stupid, but when my dad went to prison and came out, everyone that I know is because they met my dad in prison. Oh yeah, you're Tony's daughter, we met your dad in … I don't want to know! Everyone that I know has a record. It's horrible. They're all there interconnecting and all going nowhere.

But prison also leaves its sequels through the traumatism it causes. One of the young people evokes it in a poignant manner:

Donald: It's a nightmare to go into a room, the door shuts, you put your blanket on your bed, you look at the door, there's no handle, you're not going home. You have to experience that for yourself. You hear fully grown men crying in the night. I sat there and read and thought, what a waste of time! The rats were on stilts.

The nightmare continues when they come out of prison, jobless, moneyless and without any perspective for the future.

Daryl: But when they come out of prison, what have they got to go back to?

If they apply for a job, their past is prohibitive. They are thus caught in a vicious circle and fall back into delinquency. This is one concern for the young people.

Donald: They go back to the same people, the same troubles and after five or six weeks they think, well I've got no money and every time I go for an interview they say, where have you been for the last … and then someone else is saying, do you wanna come and do this … and you're like, well I do need some money.

Sally: My brother is in prison at the moment, and what you say about money, it is a real problem. My brother's been in and out and it's like what you was saying, what's he got to come out for? As you said, if he's gonna go for a job, they're gonna say oh, you've been in prison, oh my gosh. It's like, he comes and he's got no money, so his friends say, 'you wanna come and do a crime then?'.

The Media

The young people have no illusions about the role of the media which they consider as one major site of production of the stigmatising ideology for them. One young man recounts a typical series on the television where the African-Caribbean not only is a criminal but also sells out all of his accomplices.

> Donald: You must have seen 'The Bill' where there's a Black person on every week. They always get arrested, and then tell the police everyone who was involved in the crime.

As for positive heroes, they are generally acted by white actors, states one of the young men:

> Donald: We have the biggest history on the planet but most of it is lost. Bini Brown mentioned TV, which is one of the biggest brain washers we could ever come across. You can sit there and talk about the different films you've seen, of biblical stories, who was Cleopatra?
>
> Group: Elizabeth Taylor.
>
> Donald: Who was Moses?
>
> Group: Charlton Heston.
>
> Donald: Do you understand what I'm saying? All the actors was white.

With such forceful categorisation by majority society, is there any space left for other modes of group identification?

Ethnicity and Self-definition

For the sake of analysis it is useful to differentiate categorisation by the majority of society (ascription) and self-definition by the group itself. Social reality is much more complex and one needs to be vigilant to avoid a reification of the group while presenting a static image of this reality. In particular the self-definition of the group in a minority position is not unassailable by the categorisation imposed by majority society; this makes part of unequal interaction in the relation of domination (Jenkins 1997).

Donald: The people who make the big decisions are the majority, and the majority is your colour [white].

Moreover, self-definition itself is fluid and situational in relation to circumstances and differences of generation, class and sex.

The question posed here is that of ethnicity and group identification. Is there an ethnic identification among the young African-Caribbeans? What are the tenets of this ethnicity, its substance, its forms and, in particular, what are the similarities soldering the group together and the differences in relations to the Other? What does it mean for the people concerned to be young African-Caribbeans in Britain? Does it provide a basis for social action?

Colour

The young people in our group determine the first important source of identification as that of skin colour. Less than in the United States but very clearly more so than in France; partly as a consequence of the categorisation as such, and the importance attributed to colour by majority society but also because it testifies to other links and to a common myth of origin. Colour is constructed as a central signifier, sometimes independent of the family milieu. For the young people in the group there is no doubt about it.

Daryl: We may have many ideas but we have our colour as a common identity. Because at the end of the day we're Black.

Ian: When I say we're born into one and three, collective identity, I mean the colour of our skin.

For instance, Sebastian, who was brought up by white adoptive parents, clearly identifies as Black.

Sebastian: Black identity means that you have a foundation, something has been there.

For these young people the colour translates a common history, that of slavery colonisation and a remote African origin. This is their own and differentiates them clearly from the white English and other minorities. These themes are prevalent in the discourse and the preoccupation of the young African-Caribbeans.

Family, Mother

In religion and the family are to be found the two sources from which they draw their values and a notion of good and bad.

Miriam: From number one, that's from my family, mainly my mom and my church.

The family inculcates culture and tradition.

William: I was just trying to say that it starts in the home because a lot of culture and tradition as Black people ... we live here but we still have all those things.

Donald: Black children are the same, yet at the same time very different. We have different cultures, family background and home lives.

Family is considered as important and the mother is perceived as its pillar by all the young people present. She inspires at the same time love and respect. Their primary source of socialisation remains as can be expected, the family group. This is the only occasion during the whole sociological intervention process, when the group makes a specific reference to gender. Until then, no differentiation was apparent. In this instance, there is a clear emphasis placed on the mother by the whole group (barring the youngster who grew up in care and with foster parents).

Sandra: My idea of collective identity comes from my mom. I know enough to make me strong.

Donald: In my house, my dad was wash up, mow the lawn, go to the shop and my mom was the rock, the oak in the hill, wind blowing, leaves fall off and she's still there, that's my mom! My dad sat with the remote control, Guinness punch; and all the major decision-making came from my mom. If you misbehaved, she called that bloke sitting there watching the TV drinking the Guinness punch. Mums in Caribbean families are the rock.

A young woman from a mixed parentage doesn't have any doubts about her ethnic and group identity: she is Black like her mother although she was brought up in a white area.

Alice: I come from Tyseley, which is an industrial area, so there's a lot of factories there, and a lot of white people, so there wasn't much Black people there to interact with, but my mom always took me to areas populated with Black people, because of the people that she knew, so I don't know. That's how I grew up knowing Black people, because my mom knew them.

Churches and Religion

In the islands of origin, churches play a central role in the structuration of communities and the first generation has transplanted them in Britain. This is what the Black theologian explained.

Robert: If you go to Jamaica, there is a church on every street corner, there's probably a hand gun on every street corner. The people who came here in the '50s and '60s brought that religious tradition with them. Many of them chose to practise outside the mainstream Anglican Methodist churches, and found a more positive way to express themselves religiously and culturally through independent churches: New Testament Church of God, Church of God of Prophecy, Church of God in Christ.

Churches continued to figure prominently among the first generation while the young people do not seem to accord them the same importance. It is more a given in their social environment. Moreover, they address clearly modern criticisms to their parents' 'sectarian and narrow-minded' churches. For most of the people concerned, church is written in a familiar landscape and a family landscape.

Donald: Well, I was not raised in church, I am a Christian now but I was a little rough-neck back in the day. Church was just one of those places you go on a Sunday and your gran would send you.

Religion seems to be a natural baggage which is not questioned.

Sandra: I think to myself, do I know anybody that hasn't got any religious faith? Because I can honestly say that I don't know anyone that doesn't have any spirituality.

And yet some of the young people regularly frequent a church.

Culture and Music

To define themselves the young people also mention the way of being which distinguishes them from the Other: more expansive and communicative, they state that they speak with their hands, they lend more attention to their clothes and they do things with style.

> Donald: Even the way Black people walk. They put a style to everything. If a Black person is good at something, he'll add his own style to it. It could be anything.

Some comments on their part are telling about what they conceive as their identity. For instance, one of them criticises a speaker who has just gone, and another of the young people interrupts him.

> Daryl: It's a European thing to not agree with someone, and wait until they've gone to talk about them behind their back. ˚

In this instance, 'European' is contrasted with their own ethnic identity. They say that their food cannot be confused with white English cooking. They also note that most of the characteristics described above are not given any value in a cultural English framework.

> Donald: But in order to get there you have to play the game. You have to act Europe and totally disregard your ethnicity. To get by in England, you have to act Eurocentric. Totally disregard your Afro-Caribbean business and your mumbo-jumbo and your bongo drums, and talk as if you're a BBC news reader. Then you will get somewhere.

The cultural marker which is hailed as the most determining is that of Black music in which all recognise themselves and which for them constitutes an intrinsic element of their identity; moreover, it demonstrates the hegemony of Black culture. This was indisputably confirmed by the inclusion of Bob Marley in the programme of the Proms in 1998, this arch-traditional British musical institution. Music also demonstrates the existence of the communion or even of a transnational Black community in a triangle: the United States, the Caribbeans and Britain (Gilroy 1993). As soon as music is mentioned the group goes into effervescence.

Danièle: But do you think it has a particular importance for Black people? The music.

Daryl: It's something that's been down in the generations, man!

Music incarnates the glory of their triumph over the majority society which inferiorises them. It is for them a reversal of ascription.

Ian: I mean look what we've invented, soul, blues, jazz ... pop music.

Donald: Black people *are* pop music.

Alice: Music!

Music is also quoted in connection with dance.

The Carnival

In Birmingham, it is the Handsworth Carnival which constitutes the most significant yearly event for African-Caribbeans. It is an opportunity to meet, to celebrate together the common culture and especially music.

Sandra: Okay, on carnival day, you can catch a bus full of Black people and you know where they're all going. People from all sides of town. If there's any time that we're gonna come together, it will be there.

The carnival represents an important collective activity among the African-Caribbean community.

Simon: So the carnival is something which brings the Black community together.

The Carnival has a significant symbolic meaning and the young people are completely conscious of this.

Ian: Really it's just the one thing that Black people look forward to. I stopped going for a time, but it's a fact that Black people in Birmingham look forward to that. There's no national Black day for our heroes, so all we have is carnival.

The Carnival is their own thing, which also explains the disapproval vehemently expressed when Birmingham City Council proposed a change of name.

Daryl: But we just want something of our own, where we as Black people can go to.

Simon: Don't they think Black people are gonna get angry when they change it from Handsworth Carnival and call it Birmingham International Carnival?

Indeed, Handsworth is identified as an African-Caribbean area *par excellence*. It is also in that area that the urban riots of 1981–85 took place. To replace the name of Handsworth Carnival by Birmingham Carnival proposes different connotations.

The young Black find their positive models mostly in sport and show business, but they argue that it is not enough to be Black and to have made it to become a role model: those that have broken with their group of origin, and have become yes men assimilated to white elites must be rejected, such as the comic Lenny Henry or the boxer Frank Bruno. The true positive models for these young people are those which maintain their links with the African-Caribbean group and demonstrate their solidarity through helping others to succeed, for instance, the comic John Simitt.

Language

The question of language demonstrates the plasticity of the cultural content and the construction of a marker specific to young African-Caribbeans in the country of immigration of their parents. Indeed, the language of their home is generally a Creole of English spoken in their island of origin but this varies from one island to another and yet in Birmingham and in Britain most of the young African-Caribbeans know Patois which is the Creole spoken in Jamaica; they tend to know it whatever the island of origin. The use of Patois enables them to establish or consolidate an ethnic and social link to differentiate themselves from the others and to understand reggae, rap and other kinds of songs. It constitutes a code which only the in-group shares in and understands. Once again the central role of music is confirmed in its contribution to the language as Patois is most often the medium of Black music in the UK.

Daryl: Now, I know that when I want to speak to someone in patois, I can speak it. I was complimented the other day by a lady at my job, she said she loves when young people speak patois, and I was pleased.

Conclusion

Clearly the weight of racism and categorisation by majority society on the young people and their awareness of it outbalance the emphasis placed on their self-identification as a group. This reflects the power relations wherein they are caught up by which they are placed in a disadvantaged position. Although they understand the mechanisms of discrimination and prejudice, this does not dissipate their impact. On the contrary, the whole life of those young people is stamped and marred by it. Nevertheless, they do differentiate themselves culturally (to an extent), they partake of shared meanings (some of which are the result of their interaction with discriminatory practices and prejudice), the ethnic markers they select are manipulable. Their identification is at the same time individual and collective. This seems to indicate some ethnic awareness among the young African-Caribbeans (Jenkins 1997, p. 40). But this only represents one dimension of their relationship with the majority society.

Chapter Six

Meanings and Mechanisms of Action

Introduction

The dichotomy and interaction between categorisation by majority society and self-identification through a number of ethnic markers does not suffice to account for the processes of group identification among the young people concerned. The heritage of centuries of racism and inferiorisation dating back to slavery is compounded by the stigma which immigrant workers in low status and low wage jobs have suffered in Britain. This is bound to leave a mark on these young people's self-perception and the perception of society at large. The territorial basis of identification is another source of data which needs to be examined: Africa, the Caribbean, Britain, the locality, all have to be interrogated, as well as social sources of identification. Finally, the paths of action they follow will derive from the intertwining of those factors.

Unequal Interactions and Reactions

Within the structure of power relations in Britain, African-Caribbeans suffer from a dual social and 'racial' disadvantage. The deleterious effect of racist prejudice can be significant and it will affect their own group consciousness, whether they internalise it or react against it.

Alienation and Negativism

The young people adopt a critical distance towards their environment and are not prisoners of the stereotypes which are exercised towards them. However, the experience of racism and discrimination can be debilitating for them. The young African-Caribbeans have an acute feeling of powerlessness against ascription and against those who control the reins of power. Defeatism is widespread. What can one do against school underachievement, the mishandling of the police, discrimination in employment etc.?

> Daryl: I believe that, looking at the structure of somewhere like Handsworth

college, in a Black community, how many Black people are running that college? It's people from outside.

They cannot see any escape through political participation, whether it be parties or elections and none of them vote anyway. They do not believe that populations of Caribbean origin are in a position to take on collective initiatives capable of promoting the interest of African-Caribbeans. They think that the factors which divide them, such as islands of origin and churches, are more important than those that could unite them.

> Daryl: I don't understand that, because you have the same people talking about Black community then they put other islands down. Like if you're not from Jamaica then you ain't got it going.

The churches, which play an important role in the country of origin and in structuring the networks of first generations, are criticised for their closed attitude, their sectarianism in Great Britain and are not valued by the young people.

> William: It's like my mom and all of them, they think every other religion is wrong and even the people outside are wrong, it's only their church that is right.

They speak of a lack of solidarity in collective projects which makes them jealous of each other so that the success of the one is shot down rather than being celebrated as a success of the group; a kind of negativism penetrates the group.

> William: Your Black person wants to peg you down, they don't want to see you go up there, because they're still on the same level. Yeah you can, but what I'm saying is that Black people, they love to run each other down, when someone gets up there a little bit, they don't want to see them up there, they'd rather be up there themselves, or they curse them.

What is lacking is the hope of success and this brings about a kind of fatalism; on the contrary, instead of anticipating success, African-Caribbean people still expect that Blacks will fail.

> Alice: It's like we have to expect a failure. Like people expect a Black business to fail.

The young people conclude that African-Caribbeans are their own worst enemy.

> Donald: I think Black people are their own worst enemy.

This results from an internalisation of the racial category towards them and of the relation of domination stemming from their class position, slavery, colonisation and discrimination against immigrants, as Fanon (1975) and Memmi (1972) described it. This state of things is manifested in a variety of ways.

Among the first generation the common reaction was that of submission coupled with an inferiority complex.

> Robert: Yeah. Caribbean people were taught to be submissive and believe
>   that anything white was better than Black, and it still has a profound
>   effect on second generations.

The young people themselves know that they are affected by this process that undermines their confidence.

> Sandra: Yeah, so we start to think of ourselves as failures.

They are perfectly conscious of the mechanism that alienates them.

> Daryl: It's a shame because you can break a man down by taking away his
>   emotional stability. You tell him that he's dirty and stupid long enough
>   and he begins to believe it.

And yet they continue to be influenced by stereotypes towards them. One of them who did a placement at a solicitor's office was astonished to count among the clients only one African-Caribbean person, a woman, who had made a fraudulent tax declaration, whereas he was expecting to see a string of young Black delinquents coming through the practice.

> Sebastian: I worked at a solicitor's office and a barrister's chamber, and I hardly
>   saw any Black people. The majority of clients I saw were white. But
>   I had a perception that I would see a whole heap of Black people.

All were surprised to hear that the wounds inflicted to one of the speakers (the policewoman) were carried out by a young white man under the influence of drugs.

Police:	This was done by a crack head. A young man who was so high on
Officer	drugs, he lost consciousness and I wanted to get him to the hospital.
	He regained consciousness in the back of the ambulance and went
	ballistic.

William: Was this a Black guy?

| Police: | No, a white lad, about 6 feet tall. |
| Officer | |

William: See, that's good, because we have the stereotype of crack head being Black …

The young people had mixed feelings and views about the Creole language. They set it in contrast to languages of the Indian Peninsula and reproduced the dominant discourse in England a few years ago about Creole, then defined as bad English.

Sandra: See, they have their language, we lost our language. Which took away our power.

Another consequence deriving from the alienation process is their perception of the Black group as a fragmented group deprived of positive models.

Donald: We haven't really got any Black role models, the most successful Black people in this country are sports personalities, there are no actors.

They deplore the lack of social, human and identity resources among the African-Caribbeans which takes many of them into a vicious circle of poverty, delinquency, prison and drug trafficking.

William: Whereas, if you're the stereotypical Black, you seem to get more street creed and recognition and reputation.

Daryl: This is why last year a lot of the kids were getting killed. The problem is some of them try too hard to be gangsters.

Indeed, according to them those who succeed and could constitute positive models for the young people leave the inner city and leave the upper hand to dealers and troublemakers. The latter impose themselves through force and through their opulent riches, manifestations of wealth, sports cars, their gold watches, clothes of expensive labels.

> Sandra: I think it's down to self-respect and role models, that we have a lack of role models. Because everyone has to look up to someone.

> Daryl: I'm talking from the Lozells area. The problem is the big old guys standing outside the shop, smoking and you have the young people who see this. They say well, he's got a BMW ...

The young people in the group constantly stress the weaknesses of their own fragmented community and its situation of failure.

> Daryl: But I'm saying that we don't even have that. Look how long Soho Road is, and how many shops do we have?

Several times over they quote the success of Asians in order to make more evident the failure of their own group. Asians represent for them the typical example of successful communities.

> Ian: Asians stick together more than Blacks.

> Sandra: They're also more community orientated.

According to the young people, Asians are organised, demonstrate solidarity and are capable of carrying through collective initiatives.

> Sandra: Look at the top of Soho Road, you can see that temple for miles, and the people built that themselves together, for the community.

Asians occupy the economic space through their numerous shops and businesses, the political space through their representation among city councillors and the professional space as doctors, dentists and solicitors. This is how they are perceived by the young Blacks group.

> Donald: Asian people work hard and stick together. Where I live, in Alum Rock, everywhere, the doctor, the dentist, the butcher, the baker, the candlestick maker [group laughs], are all Asian.

On the one hand the young African-Caribbeans attribute the success of Asians to their community mobilisation, on the other hand to advantages that are supposed to make it easier for them.

Sandra: At the end of the day, if they need a loan from the bank. If me and him went to the bank and said, we've got our plan set out, ready, what are you saying, give us a grand, they would laugh. Now an Indian man walks in there, a white man walks in there and it's, 'how much do you need'?

Young people express thus their relative frustration: they brush aside the presence of city councillors who are African-Caribbean, arguing that they are merely token Blacks and do not regard as of any significance the fact that the first ethnic minority councillor was an African-Caribbean. They also deny the existence of the community and community networks of any sort among the African-Caribbeans.

Donald: We are a bunch of no-nation people. We have no base.

Alice: The way we are, there's no structure, nothing to stand on in the Black community. They've got no aim, nothing in front of them, nothing behind them.

The ultimate proof of this state of things, according to the young people, is the cancellation of the Handsworth carnival last year because the African-Caribbean community was not able to bring together sufficient funding so that it could take place.

Sally: Well, basically, the community didn't help, and finances were low.

They express indignation at having to 'whiten' themselves to have the same chances as white British. They are conscious that they need to behave according to English cultural norms and get rid of their 'natural way of being', in other words to play a role; moreover, the strength of the stereotype imposes on them behaviours that will not leave any space for their own culture.

Donald: Like, you know, when you're walking and there's a white person in front of you, usually a woman, and you're walking at pace, and you think, 'I hope she doesn't turn left', and she turns left, 'I hope she doesn't cross the zebra crossing', and she does …I just run past.

Denise: So think that stereotypes prevent us from moving forward and we often live our own stereotypes.

They feel that they are condemned as victims.

Resistance

It is manifest that the young people in our sociological intervention group, while recognising the weight of negative stereotypes, do not conform to them. They clearly reject the option of violence, whether it be riots or delinquency. Some have been delinquents and some have been in jail, but they managed to overcome this handicap. Even though they are interested in music and several of them are musicians, they also study. Several of them tried to take a second chance by preparing their 'A' levels in the evening or on a part-time basis in further education colleges.

> Denise: Now, what I've found is that a lot of Black people go to university
>   as mature students, which means they skip the stage of A levels, but
>   do access courses which are very difficult, and go on to do degrees.

Up until 1998 the existence of grants, although insufficient, had been useful in helping them to work towards a qualification but the whole situation is changing to the detriment of disadvantaged groups. The young people concerned make all possible efforts to overcome obstacles but they identify the central question for young African-Caribbeans as a valorisation of their culture and the history of Black people. They would derive from it a positive image and a greater confidence in their capacity for action. They will also gain a space of dignity and an identity resource that would help them to distance themselves from the stigma affecting them (Lapeyronnie 1993). The main theme they pursue is that of negritude, oppression and cultural resistance.

> Donald: Black people haven't got enough self-worth. I don't think they
>   believe in themselves [group agrees]. Most of what I learned about
>   Black history wasn't at school, you only learn about European history
>   at school and white contribution to society. So you're taught at school
>   to be racist. I don't mean Black people but the majority of people in
>   this country are. You only learn about white contributions to society.
>   But if you knew that the numerical system was made by Black people,
>   the alphabet, the first architects, scientists, doctors were all Black
>   people, I think Black people would sit up and be like, 'wait, didn't it
>   all start from chains and being chased through some forests
>   somewhere?'

For one of them it is prison, one of the worst consequences of the Black condition, which enabled him to learn about Black history.

> Larry: I started reading books, mainly when I was in jail. That's how I've looked into Black history.

The Black theologian who came as a speaker speaks of a rite of passage through prison, quoting the experience of leaders like Marcus Garvey, Martin Luther King, Nelson Mandela.

> Robert: Yeah, and that's an important point, cause when we think of some of the major Black male figures, prison has been a place of conversion and re-orientation, you can think of Malcom X, Marcus Garvey, even Nelson Mandela. And Martin Luther King wrote some of his best letters from prison. So, prison is actually a 'rite of passage' in many Black communities, not just here but in the US, it's where people get re-focused.

The young people's interest for Black theology results from the same process, that is a rereading of the Bible and an exegesis making a full place for Africans. This theology is considered as a tool of liberation against the alienation of the dominant ideology which, among others, portrays Jesus Christ and all the important characters with blonde hair and blue eyes. Hence their acute interest in the speech of the Black theologian, who was the first speaker to come. Questions did not stop during that session. The young people wanted to know more. The generation of young people brought up on British soil will not accept everything and take it lying down like their parents, as they emphasised several times. For their parents, status is derived from the way they would be perceived in their society of origin, so that discrimination and low wages assume a secondary importance. For young people who grew up in Britain, this is not the case as their status is determined from within British society.

> Larry: With my dad it was the fact that being Black in a white community, you've got to do the right thing or else they will pick on you. But with me it's flipped over, I look at the police the opposite way, not from his view.

Music plays a central role in the cultural resistance of African-Caribbeans. On the one hand it is a source of pride because young Blacks are conscious of the indisputable Black prevalence in this domain, particularly in the Anglo-Saxon world.

On the other hand, the lyrics themselves feed into the culture of resistance. The music contributes to weave a network of Black people around the Atlantic Ocean. As a summary, music enables them to reverse ascription. Finally, the young Blacks defend the notion of solidarity with the Third World against imperialism and multinational companies. They promote the respect of primitive civilisations and the control of their own natural resources by autochthonous populations in developing countries. What they put forward, first and foremost, are universal moral values.

Integration and Modernity

While they claim their own ethnic identity, young African-Caribbeans also state that they belong to British society. Their ethnicity does not include animosity towards the white English and they do not feel that they have to keep separate.

> Miriam: My mom still thinks it's wrong for a Black woman to go out with a white man, and I'm saying to her, things have changed. She has a different perspective to what I have.

The British Option

They strongly reject the pan-Africanist option which was offered to them by one of the speakers. Firstly because they detect in it an anti-white attitude. One mentions his white foster parents, another a white partner or white friends. What they describe is a close incorporation with British society.

> William: I just can't deal with people like that, cos if I did that to my white friends, they'd think I've gone crazy. And I was raised by white people, I'm not gonna look down on them. Eleven years I was raised by white people, you can't tarnish everyone the same.

> Daryl: I wonder if I'd said to him that I have a white partner, he would have brought out the oil and …

> Larry: What about my white girlfriend and my four daughters who are half white?

They also think that Africa remains very remote in their history and from their present experience. It cannot provide an adequate answer to the identity question, neither alone nor as a main component.

> Daryl: Because we can talk about Africa until you're blue in the face, but what are you doing in the local community? We're discussing Birmingham, and he's doing a of tour of Nibingi.

They do not seem to find a satisfactory answer to that question in the island of origin either.

> Sandra: Even in the Caribbean, it isn't our home.

The conclusion which they draw is that they belong to Britain, albeit sometimes by default.

> Donald: I think all of us in this room was born in England, and we've taken on English personalities. None of us really act African any more, so when you talk about being African, we sit here thinking, in what ways? We think European really. We have extra bits of African history that we all know, but we think European.

This view is supported by John Simmitt's comments, who finds it very difficult to communicate his Black British humour to North American audiences.

> Ian: There is a difference between the Black Americans and the English Blacks.

The Local Dimension

However, more than an identification to Britain, what the young people express is an attachment to the locality, the town, the area.

> Alice: I don't think we care much for England in a sense really. The only thing I've got is where we live, the actual area I'm from.

When they meet John Simmitt, the Black comic from Handsworth, they demonstrate a perfect communion with him and they state their appreciation of the fact that he remained in the region rather than settle in London.

> Danièle: Does John represent a role model for you? We've been talking a lot about role models in the past sessions.

Sandra: I suppose yes. He's successful, and he's from Birmingham too.

Danièle: It's important that he's from Birmingham?

Sebastian: Definitely.

The problems which are close to their hearts are those of the area.

Daryl: But my problem is that I live in the Newtown area, what is he doing? What is he doing for people when they come out [of prison]? To me he had no substantial answers.

In this, they are similar to their white peers for whom the local dimension is also the most significant one, for instance in the shape of allegiance to a football team.

J. Simmitt: For white guys it's quite natural to support a local team, it's the same localisation thing. You support the local crowd rather than the fact of whether they ever win anything.

A Social Identification

The young people in the group also expressed a social identification. They are integrated into British society along its social cleavages and they know where they belong, as they say, on the side of the poor and the powerless. As Donald said to Ray Griffiths, trade union officer:

Donald: I haven't got a problem talking to you because I can tell that you are working class.

However, the identification is not principally formulated in terms of organised class solidarity; trade unions fail to attract their interest or their trust. The young people do not feel concerned as they have not yet had a job, or only very precarious jobs.

Sandra: The main issue is getting a job first. TUs come afterwards.

This is what they say without qualms to the trade union speaker; one of them did not even know whether his parents were members of a trade union, whereas in fact they had worked all their lives in a corporation with a closed shop.

Larry: My mom and dad have worked every day since they set foot in this country. But I don't know if they were members of TUs. They both worked for British Telecom, GPO.

TU
Officer: Well, the GPO was TU organised, it was a condition of employment.

On the other hand, they are in perfect agreement with the representative of a residents' association of a deprived white area talking to them about his efforts to regenerate the area. They see in it the exact counterpart of the inner city area where some of them live. They compare point for point the indicators of spiritual, moral and material deprivation on both sites. They almost make a sociological analysis: single teenage motherhood, delinquency, poverty, dirt, stigmatisation of the area. The list is long, and also includes feelings of insecurity, drugs, brawls, the lack of meeting places, no facilities for young people, no feeling of belonging, no project or meaning, the experience of prison and its vicious circle, joblessness, no support, no long-term project, but instead, a request for immediate results. The problem of racism is not even raised. The young people notice that the white area of Chelmsley Wood and the inner city area of Newtown are similar. Both have their contingent of single mothers.

Donald: The nickname for Chelmsley Wood at the moment, 'bastard city'. Cos if you look at any block of flats on Chelmsley Wood, guarantee the majority of people who live in the flats are single mothers who are about 17 or 18, go clubbing, and are going nowhere.

Daryl: It's like, I live in Newtown and what's happening now is a lot of fixing up in Newtown. Great! But I think it could be becoming like Chelmsley Wood cos there's a lot of single parents and there's a lot of crime.

The idleness of the young people and the lack of facilities in those areas entail a negative use of their energy.

Miriam: The thing as well, there's a lack of things to do in Chelmsley Wood and that's why they're going off and doing what they wanna do.

Donald: Our idea of having a good time when we were bored, when I was about 13, 14, was to throw bricks at cars going past by the subway. Sometimes we used to phone up the police and get them to come to cul-de-sacs and just hammer the car. That was our way of enjoyment. We had so much energy, and it was always used in a negative way.

In both areas the role model is that of the gangster.

Larry: The most successful people in the inner city are the hoodlums, the fighters, the dealers. In any area, doesn't matter if it's white or Black.

In the same way Newtown residents do not feel that they are directly concerned by urban regeneration projects because their participation is not called upon.

Daryl: The problems of living in Newtown is they've got over £50 million but it's not involving the local people in building up the area. You can have wonderful trees and they will cut them down. It's not the fact that it's collecting rubbish, it's the fact that they've been given something to do. So instead of someone else doing it, it's like your sweat and toil.

The young people accuse the urban structure which is deemed to aggravate the case of the areas in question.

Donald: I was there waving my flag when the shopping centre was built on Chelmsley Wood. I think that the way it's designed, it could only breed crime.

Danièle: Why do you think it breeds crime?

Donald: Just the shape ... have you ever been there?

As a summary one of the young people finds an incomparable formula which demonstrates to what extent they are conscious of a social identification. Not only do they draw parallels between the Black and the poor white classes, but they demonstrate that the reverse is also true.

Donald: But Chelmsley Wood is sort of like the Blacks of Solihull. The rest of Solihull is really nice.

The common enemy leaves no doubt, it is the rich, the bourgeois, those who control economic power, the judiciary and political power.

Donald: Of course. If you're a professional person, say on TV or in a band, and you want some class A drugs, you don't have to go down a dirty street. You make a phone call, someone drops it off, pure. But if you're working class and you do some menial task, and you want that same drug, you've got to go out and earn the shillings. So you don't have to put yourself in the frame if you got a decent job.

The young people condemn the British ruling class which would like to believe, and make believe, that Britain is still a great power, whereas they perceive it in such a state of collapse compared to other European countries which some of the young people have visited. The political class is held as hypocritical because it makes promises which it does not keep and does not have the faintest idea what a life of poverty and deprivation can mean; the same can be said of the Solihull magistrates, in a rich area, who condemn small delinquents.

> William: I think politicians have a bad attitude, like the sound of their own voice and are really ignorant.

The government and the media are also held as responsible.

> Donald: The media and the government are the two most powerful bodies in this country.

This indifference, this diffidence or this hostility towards institutions is not only an attribute of young African-Caribbeans; young white English of humble background share them. For the young Blacks the enemy is also the multinationals which trample on the interest of people and are ready to do anything in pursuit of their sacred profits.

> Ian: The rich get richer and the poor get poorer?

The young people are indignant in the face of the unequal distribution of riches in a static society which lives off the myth of imperial superiority and impedes all social mobility for young African-Caribbeans.

Capacity for Action

From the beginning it is clear that the collective capacity for action of the young African-Caribbeans is limited, as they deny the existence or significance of networks and community associations and brush aside any classical mode of collective action through trade unions or political parties. Their relationship

to institutions is negative: no compromise with the police, an implacable
diffidence towards the political apparatus and disillusionment towards school.

> Donald: I don't think it makes a difference who you vote for, or whether you
>   vote or not. The parties are the same in my eyes, no matter who
>   wins the election, they all tell lies.

For example, the young people criticise the school system which places them,
they say, in a situation of failure. There is no recognition of their value,
discrimination, inferiorisation, hierarchy of cultures. They know practically
no Black teacher nor programmes taking into account the history of Black
people.

> Sebastian: They are not educated about themselves, i.e. Black history and so
>   forth. The educational system that we're in, does not necessarily
>   cater for us. Therefore, either we adapt or we drop out.

Their total rejection of politics or political parties and of the vote is
accompanied with an astonishing ignorance of the way the political system
functions. They did not even know who John Prescott was (then deputy leader
of the Labour Party) just prior to the general elections which brought the
Labour Party to government. The young people were incapable of putting
forward claims as a group to the leader of the City Council who came to
speak to them.

> Donald: That would never work with her.

Their positive identification and their preferential options are situated on the
local level, such as participation in a residents' associations, work with a youth
group; and yet, although they claim to be keen on the promotion of Black
people, they often express their defeatism and negativism in the face of their
racial and social handicap.

The Resources for Action

The researchers in the sociological intervention group called the young people's
attention to the fact that they spend much time lamenting and little time
discussing the possibility of action. On the whole, they prefer to opt for cultural
or individual modes of action. They stress the importance of teaching the
history of Black people which would enhance their self-image and confidence,

but they do not know how to achieve this objective and are not ready to mobilise in a collective manner for that purpose. Nevertheless, some of them seriously asked the question of the possibility of action.

Daryl: Since I've been doing this, I've thought about one thing, what am I doing as a Black person? I want to be productive in my area, and I ask myself, 'what can I do?' I listen to people talk, but they're not doing anything.

They debated what is the most necessary thing. First of all, to know one's history, posited one of them.

Sebastian: I think that knowing your history is essential. If we all have the same agenda, you can move forward. If we're split up, we can't move together.

Others argued that one of the main objective was to regain self-esteem, and one way to do it is education.

Sebastian: Self-respect is lacking in our young people today. If I don't respect myself, how can I respect you?

Sandra: I think the key is education, because if you know about these things, you have more pride in yourself.

The young Blacks also stressed that they have a great need for better solidarity.

Donald: What I think Black people in this country need more than any other race of people, is solidarity between their own people. And, professional Black people helping other Black people, and bringing money back to the Black community, to help other Black people to prosper. The Black people who are successful, don't come back to the Black community.

One of the solutions proposed is the creation of meeting places to consolidate the community and group activities.

Daryl: Yeah, just the fact that there is a pub there, there's a sense of community, somewhere people can socialise. In Newtown they have an evening youth club and you can see them, when someone is refused entrance, you can see how upset the kids are, because it's something for them to do. This is why Theresa Stewart needs to listen to this. Simply things like that can build confidence, cos they have something to do. Instead of hanging around the streets they can go to the youth clubs.

Finally, they must also convince the rest of the population and this task is underlined as the most difficult one.

Donald: We have to convince ourselves of who we are, where we are and where we're going, and then convince the rest of the population. I think it's more stressful now that I've been here today, than it ever has been.

The researchers propose to them the thesis of a disadvantage which is coupled with an advantage compared to their English, white counterparts.

The disadvantage is apparent and nobody questions it. They share with their white peers social disadvantage, which is itself multiplied by a racial disadvantage, i.e. stereotype, racism and discrimination. However, they wonder what advantages they may have. Researchers quote their ethnic identity underpinned by a clear group identification. Secondly, the distance from the majority of society, that of the stranger, which awards them a superior capacity of analysis. Finally, they enjoy community networks from which they benefit in many ways. Those very networks which they denied existed and are yet quite manifest: churches, family networks, conviviality in marking events of life (marriages, burials, birth, christening). Those networks extend overseas. The young people, at first surprised, discussed those propositions point by point. In the first place, tackling the question of identity, they fairly rapidly concluded that they do benefit from a clear consciousness of their Black identity.

Sebastian: Black identity means that you have a foundation, something has been there.

Denise: How many times do you walk into a room full of white people and look for the first Black person, and nod your head when you see them.

Danièle: So there is a consciousness of a common experience. An identity.

Donald: I'll agree with that.

In addition this collective identity is perceived as a neat advantage.

Donald: Yes, cos when you know where you're from, and you realise how many good things Black people have achieved in the past you feel a pride in yourself, you even walk different. You even speak to people different, you're more calm.

The group still hesitated to recognise the existence of community networks amongst Blacks while they kept comparing this deficiency to networks existing amongst Asians; but eventually they accepted that 'there was something' and remembered how their parents settled into Britain.

Daryl: When we came here historically, things weren't going down in some of the churches, and Black people got together and formed their own churches. So they formed a power base in the community, through the church.

They compare themselves to the majority population in the same socioeconomic strata.

Sandra: Yeah, but Danièle is comparing us to the white community, and if you're comparing the Black and white community, there is more sense of a community within the Black community, even though it's breaking down.

Alice: I think Black people have more pride in themselves.

The young people also demonstrate a very modern individualism in their aspiration and personal project. They think of themselves as single, autonomous individuals. Moreover, most of them have links with the world overseas. They partake of networks extending beyond the seas which enable them to travel and increase their modern cosmopolitan quality.

Donald: We're always told that other European countries are poorer than us, but I went to Denmark last year and the taxi drivers drive top of the range Mercedes! There was no rubbish, no poor people. I was surprised. In a lot of ways England is behind and it's sort of a blinkered vision in England.

The young people, after discussing it, agree with the hypothesis proposed by the researchers and conclude that this gives them greater confidence in their capacity of action.

Sandra: If you're determined enough to go for what you want, society is
            gonna be saying no, the white dominant society will be saying, no.
            But if we're determined to go there, we'll fight for it.

The Path of Action

When the possible orientations of action are deciphered, three paths are
identified by the young people.

1) Community work which a few choose to pursue: youth worker in a
   community centre for young African-Caribbeans or playgroup leader
   among African-Caribbean children and counsellor among young African-
   Caribbeans in prison. During the work of the sociological intervention
   group, one of the young people obtained a job in this area and has therefore
   begun to realise his own project.

Daryl: Okay, I do prison ministry and what I want to do is not just visit the
            people in prison for a chat, but set up something for when they come
            out, so they don't go back to the same old ways. You need to do
            something so the people stop committing crimes. You need to
            approach them and ask what the problem is. 'Oh, we ain't got no
            jobs, we ain't got nowhere to play.' You need to approach these
            things in a logical manner and say right, 'What you need to do is get
            together as a body and do something about it.' Cos at the end of the
            day the one thing the council doesn't like is a lot of angry people.

Sally: Well, I'd like to do work in the community. Yeah, I want to work
            with young people. Working in youth clubs ... teenagers.

One of the young people declared that he wanted to put an end to the
constant lamentation and replace it by the organisation of Black people
for the purpose of action.

Daryl: No, it's like this. I work in Newtown for Burberry Park, I want to
            start some group work. I don't want to be sitting here saying moan,
            moan, moan and going home and doing nothing. I'm doing something
            and it starts off as a little thing. At the end of the day, people might
            criticise and condemn, but I want to turn round and ask the next
            man to meet me half way, cos that is the only way we're gonna end
            up doing something as a Black people, because we're always talking
            about us Black people as unorganised, it's time to get out of that

rubbish and start organising ourselves, because if we don't do it nobody is gonna do it for us. You need to start doing and stop chatting about it. I have my own ideas, I want to apply for a grant so that I can get myself a keyboard and start doing vocal workshops in Youth Clubs. But it's such a fight to get the money.

2) The penetration of institutions. One of the young people wants to become a teacher in the inner city while another want to be an educational psychologist or a solicitor.

Simon: My preferred option would be to work from within the system. I hope to be a teacher and therefore I would be in a school. Well, I would like to be a role model. I like the idea of maybe working in an all Black school one day, teaching subjects like Black history, as part of the curriculum. I think the key is education, because if you know about these things, you have more pride in yourself.

Sebastian: Or even do law.

Danièle: Why would you do law?

Sebastian: Because there's too many Black people being wrongly accused of things and also getting killed.

3) Occupation of the public space, the media or *haute couture*, to make a name, become a positive model and give a chance to other young Blacks.

Ian: I wanna be known, I want Black people to follow my role. I've always said that. I want to be one of the first Black people to have a fashion house in Paris. I want my fashion business to be run by Black people in Paris.

Danièle: So what will you promote when you're a designer?

Ian: Black models.

Danièle: Black means African-Caribbean ... it doesn't mean Asian?

Ian: No.

They underlined that it is not enough to succeed and hope that this positive model will inspire others. One constantly needs to make a special effort to promote the group in the area one has chosen.

The Triangle of Ethnicity

Fundamentally the question asked by the young Blacks is how to thrive individually and realise a personal project while integrating ethnicity and community on the one hand, modernity and Britannity on the other hand, forming a triangle of ethnicity (Wieviorka 1993). The itinerary followed is not the same for all, it circulates between the three following poles:

1) belonging to the Black collectivity and a group identity;
2) participation in British society;
3) developing as an individual.

Ethnic   British

community   society

Subject

The world map of those young people is traced by one member of the group.

> Sandra: As far I see, this is a map of what is required for life. Number one is like collective identity, and how you fit in the Black community. Number two, the individual and action, that's how we fit into the larger community, as in British, world or European community. Number three, that represents personal goals, aspirations, as in somehow trying to get a balance between the three. That's it.

It's not a question of making one single choice between one pole or the other. All the young people indicate that all three are important, but all do not propose to follow the same itinerary. One must be integrated with one's own group and at the same time with the majority society, states one of the young people.

> Donald: We need to be able to fit in with our social group, but also with the group who is oppressing us.

'If I was only an individual integrated to the majority society without recognising my group of origin I would be a Bounty,' he adds with contempt.

> Donald: If a Black person was to just do two and three, and ignore one, he would be a middle class yuppie type person, and he wouldn't be able to act Black, he'd have to act white. A Bounty is a chocolate

bar with white coconut inside. He'd have to act completely white to go up the ladder.

On the other hand he wants to enjoy the advantages of modern society, such as a car, and a good house.

> Donald: I would take in one and two, because greed is … the devil is sitting on my shoulder. I do want a nice car and I do want a nice house.

A young woman stresses that roots have to be the departure point in order to ensure solid bases.

> Sebastian: But personally, I think that to survive in number two, you need to know who you are. You start with number two, and you'll get lost. So you start with number one.

In fact the young people blend their multiple identities and select the relevant markers according to the situation.

> William: All the time. I work in a predominantly white environment, I can break into patois now and again, but, I can't be myself. I can't talk slang, because they wouldn't understand. Then when I go home and I'm mixing with friends, I'm like, I change.

> Alice: I think we have to be a mixture of all of them. You have to believe that we can achieve them, or that we are achieving them. So in order to deal with the person standing over there we bring number two into play, to talk to the person over there we use number one. I don't think it can be separated from us. They're too complex.

> Donald: Asians do it all the time. You have to be strong minded, play the game, smile, be cunning, be devious, know when to stop and when to carry on. You have to be everything, or most things. An all-rounder. If life is like a game of baseball, you can't just be the pitcher, you've got to be fielding, pitching, batting, and also catching the curve ball behind the batsman.

However, the challenge is not easy because many constraints intervene.

> Alice: Most the time you get rejected from all three. Because you're not able to produce anything, because no one's giving you the chance, and at home, no one wants to know you because you've stepped

away from them to try and get to number three. But because you've stepped away from them, they say you can't come back to number one, and when you're at number two, because you're Black, you haven't got the rights. So, you're sort of dancing around the middle, landing on your head all the time, because you're not accepted anywhere. I think I'd describe myself as a bad tennis game, there's someone who keeps serving but the other person can't receive.

Danièle: Where are you serving from?

Alice: Anywhere. I'm just trying. I understand number one to a certain extent. I know enough to get by. Number two, if someone wants to challenge me then, I'll give as good as I can get. I'm always trying to get to number three but ... I'm never actually there at one of them.

The role of the researchers is clearly recognised in the process taken up by the young African-Caribbeans.

Donald: Yeah, but from you creating this research, we had a conversation amongst ourselves and got a greater knowledge about ourselves from speaking to each other.

The finest conclusions to this identity question is provided by one of the young people.

Daryl: If you say, 'I am Black, because the society decided that I am Black,' it's too bad. If you say 'I am Black because the Black people decide that I am Black', it's a little bit better. But it's not perfect. If you say, 'I am Black also because I decide to behave as a Black, then ...'.

The rest is left to one's imagination.

Conclusion

The young people in the sociological intervention group are well aware of their individual and collective predicament due to the double weight of racial and social disadvantage. They acknowledge the alienation they are caught in while also challenging it and proposing measures to improve their collective self-image. They do not hesitate to identify with all underprivileged social groups, including white ones, against the rich and the powerful. They are not torn between their potential origins: the Caribbean, Africa, Britain but on the contrary they are capable of integrating diverse inputs into their identity make-up. However, in the last analysis, they state that they are British, and belong more precisely to a specific locality in Britain while partaking of transnational connections. They espouse the values of modernity and individualism. Sceptical about the capacity of collective action emanating from their group, they nonetheless identify the paths of action to promote the individual and the group of African-Caribbean origin; these include community work, the penetration of institutions and the occupation of the public space. Finally, their main preoccupation is how to realise themselves as subjects, within the 'triangle of ethnicity'.

Conclusions

What this research brings out in the first place is the determining role of racism in shaping the lives of the people concerned: it is recurrent, pervasive, pernicious and often deleterious. Three areas are sharply marked by it according to the young people's experience; school, the police and judiciary, and the media. These seem to combine for an augmentation of discriminatory practices in employment. But this population also experiences racial prejudice in all aspects of everyday interaction with majority society. They formulate their group identification within this constraint to which is added the class structure to which they belong and the social deprivation they suffer.

It would be more appropriate to speak of group identifications in the plural rather than the singular where the young African-Caribbeans are concerned. Consciousness of self is expressed through an awareness of colour doubtlessly also determined by the importance accorded colour in British society. Among ethnic markers they quote the significance of their mothers, religious and cultural traits (of which the central one is music) and finally, language, signalling the Patois of Jamaica as a distinctive means of communication whatever the island of origin. Another feature of the group they identify is its lack of strong community networks, which they contrast to what they perceive as dense and powerful Asian communities. They link their group fragmentation to its low self-esteem resulting from slavery and colonialism.

The answer they propose to this situation is an exegesis of their history and culture restoring their full value from which pride in oneself would derive. However, the young people also express a strong social identification with those who belong to the same social milieu, thus totally denying the prevalence of a Black and white divide. Their territorial identification is very clear: they squarely define themselves as British with 'extra bits of African history'; they reveal a strong attachment to their locality, town or neighbourhood, while relating to cosmopolitan references, through their family or community networks which are there although not so noticeable or institutionalised as those of other groups, and through music.

Since our first meeting, the young people have demonstrated great lucidity about their situation and the functioning of the surrounding society. For them the theme of violence is not pertinent; they do not speak about it, they are not interested in it, they do not think that it is their problem, it is the problem of the majority society. Statistics seem to corroborate their feeling since they belie vigorously the image which runs through the media and public opinion: that of the young Black as the archetypical violent and delinquent mugger. Statistics reveal that the rate of delinquency and crime is clearly higher in white outer ring areas than in the inner city.

The young people abundantly discuss racism and discrimination which victimise them, and their debilitating effects. They then manifest a strong social identification along the cleavages of British society. They place themselves in the camp of the people who are dominated and excluded, the poor and the powerless, on the same level as white people of a comparable socioeconomic milieu. There is no doubt in their eyes that the racial handicap is doubled with social handicap. According to them, one also needs to add a disadvantage intrinsic to their own group: the lack of solidarity and community actions which parallels the lack of knowledge of their own history. They state that collective action in a concerted manner would be necessary and that a revalorisation of their ethnicity would help to fight the failure syndrome among Blacks.

The young people find several sources of identification which they integrate as a group and as individuals drawing upon myths of origin, history, surrounding society, and different territorial spaces. And yet, while manifesting a modern cosmopolitan universalist quality, they are not 'deterritorialised'. The notion of youths 'between two cultures' torn by conflicting loyalties and cultures certainly does not apply to them, either. Nor does the notion of disintegration, of a lumpen subculture. The concepts of transnationalised segmented cultural spaces and of cultural cumulative causation could be usually extended to the young African-Caribbeans in Britain (Faist 1999). They are no longer part of the era marked by tradition, customs, strong norms and national values. They call upon more universal values: opposition to racism, respect for people's indigenous culture and resources against the bulldozer of multinational companies, the ethics of defending the poor and deprived against corrupt and deceitful political power. Their bases for action are not trade unions, class, or political parties. The question they ask more pressingly is not 'how can we organise as a group to increase our capacity for action?' but 'how can I act as an individual to further my interest as well as the group's interest?' They utilise a variety of registers, code, even languages to navigate among the reefs of life and society, and switch or change according to the situation. They are at the same time autonomous and capable of critical analysis while lacking in sufficient power and confidence.

The work of the group through sociological intervention led them to a better awareness of three important elements:

1) their superiority *vis à vis* the whites of the same socioeconomic milieu, thanks to their critical distance and their capacity for analysis;
2) the strength of their ethnic and of their cultural and identity resources, partly obscured by domination; the proof of it is music, which all of them are proud of but where the Blacks create and the whites sell. They still perceive it as an advantage over and above their white counterparts;
3) their community and family international networks, on which they can rely without even noticing it.

Why, despite this baggage, does their capacity for action remain limited? This can be explained by several factors:

1) racism, discrimination and domination remain crushing;
2) a certain degree of alienation leads them to internalise the failure syndrome;
3) the mode of functioning of British society, proposes to them only two possible courses of action:
   - individual action directed at personal success which mostly the middle-class can pursue;
   - collective action written in a very structured mode of community on the Asian model.

This dichotomy does not make a space for Black networks which are situated in between the two, along a community mode which is different. Moreover, the young Blacks are similar to their white counterparts and pursue individual strategies which supplant collective strategies. However, this conjuncture which limits the capacity of collective action favours the capacity for individual action of the members of the group. The capacity for action is fortified by group identification and community roots.

APPENDICES

Appendix I

Violence in Birmingham

Violence in the Public Domain

Violence in the public domain was mostly manifested through the so-called 'urban riots' of the 1980s. The riots were the most spectacular outburst of violence, particularly in Handsworth, Lozells and in the city centre, which projected Birmingham into the news headlines in 1981 and 1985, alongside other industrial towns. They mostly involved ethnic minority youths. These riots have been the subject of a high-level public inquiry and have been much researched (see Chapter One). However, the epoch of the great riots appears to be over. In the 1990s there are sometimes mini-riots when minor problems degenerate into a confrontation with the police in a particular area of the town. Mini-riots occasionally take place in ethnic minority areas but are generally resolved speedily. In Saltley, for instance, at the beginning of 1996 the police were putting parking tickets on cars that were parked along the main streets which belonged to Kashmiri shopkeepers. It turned into a real battle between young people of Kashmiri origin and the police but it did not last or spread.

Where young people are concerned, violence in schools seems to have increased in the last 10 years, although it is difficult to assess its progression. Teachers' trade unions indicate that in Birmingham, one teacher per week is a victim of a serious physical attack, at the hands of pupils or parents (Birmingham City Council Community Safety Strategy, estimated 1989). This violence can be that of pupils among themselves, pupils against teachers or can involve people from outside the school. The situation in Birmingham is representative of what happens at a national level in this domain. There are 480 primary and secondary schools in Birmingham, 160,000 pupils and between 10,000 and 15,000 teachers and other school employees. This does not include colleges of further education (Hill 1996; Anderson and King 1996). The increase in violence at school led the authorities to set up a Working Party on this question in Birmingham in May 1996. Nationwide, teachers trade unions have launched a national investigation as a consequence of the murder of a headteacher who was attempting to break apart two young boys fighting each other.

Football hooliganism is to be found in Birmingham (as in other British cities) which is in possession of two stadiums and teams, Aston Villa and Birmingham City. In addition, West Bromwich Albion is situated just on the border of the city and Coventry City 20 miles away. Violence associated with football may take place in the stadiums or outside. For instance the Zulu Warriors, in Stechford, Lea Hall, Shard End, have organised battles between supporters of Birmingham City and those supporting Millwall, through the use of mobile telephones. Racist gangs (such as Combat 18) also infiltrate football supporters in order to recruit them. However, racist insults are forbidden by law during football matches in Britain. In addition to incidents revolving around football, on Friday and Saturday night brawls regularly break out when pubs close in some areas of the town, for instance in Chelmsley Wood, Four Dwellings, Kingstanding, Pype Hayes etc. The people involved are mostly young white British.

'Taxing' and steaming are a specific kind of petty crime. In public transport what may happen is that a group of young people go to the upper deck of the bus and 'taxes' its passengers. Most of the perpetrators and victims are young people at school or of school age. These incidents take place in buses which transport young people between the school and their house or in the city centre where they change bus. Most of the time they are young males but sometimes also young females. The term 'steaming' is also used when one group walks into a shop and raids it in front of the shopkeeper, who is rendered powerless by numbers. The discourse used by the young people attempts to legitimate those activities. According to the police, other types of theft and robbery are more often accompanied with violence than previously. The police speak of an ethnic division of the work. For instance, according to the police, Black or white people steal cars and Asians send them to the Indian subcontinent to sell them. However, this has not been demonstrated by research or statistics. Women from the Asian peninsula, who wear heavy golden jewels are often victims of theft in the street (Inspector Rees 1996).

There are also a few cases of violent incidents amongst and between ethnic groups. For instance, gangs of young Pakistanis and Bangladeshis fought in the street in the Aston area. As a consequence the police intervened. The origins of the conflict are not clear. What is unusual is that this kind of problem was not solved or regulated within the communities by the elders, as generally happens. Amongst the population of Caribbean origin, Caribbean Ragga involves the 'Yardies', godfathers of drugs-trafficking in the 1920s, who rule through firearms. A number of incidents took place in Handsworth, which entailed five murders. Ragga evenings (from 'Ragga-Muffin', 'street urchins') are popular mostly among young Caribbeans who take 'Yardies' as a model. This music expresses the philosophy that underpins it through its lyrics: it glorifies riches, possessions, women and having a good time.

Racism gives rise to a multiplicity of actions which are not all physical attacks. Threatening letters, rubbish or excrement in letter boxes, graffiti, insults, vandalism, setting fire to letter boxes outdoors and, more rarely, setting fire to people all take place. The British Crime Survey evaluates that 730,000 crimes involve victims who are Asian and Afro-Caribbean out of which 13,000 (which means one in six) are deemed to have a racist character. One quarter of those are physical attacks and two-fifths are threats (Maung and Mirlees-Black 1994). These figures do not take into account minor incidents against minorities which are most common in areas (in homes and public spaces) such as in Four Dwellings in Quinton, Wiley Birch in Kingstanding, Chelmsley Wood, Castle Vale, Northfield and around football stadiums. They may also take place at places of work. Incidents of this kind are still happening on a regular basis now. But racist neo-fascist gangs are not to be found in an organised and structured manner as was the case 15 years ago.

Populations involved in the above-mentioned events are mostly young males who come from a deprived social background. There are groups who do not meet this description and, in particular, those perpetrating racist aggression, who may be older and drawn from different social strata. There are also some girls' gangs in cases of 'taxing' and 'steaming'. Half of the crime and two-thirds of thefts are perpetrated by people younger than 21 (Birmingham City Council, Community Safety Strategy, estimated 1989). Crimes with a racist character are mostly committed by young males and by people unknown to the victims (six out of 10 for Afro-Caribbeans and seven out of 10 for Asians). With regard to Asian victims, three quarters of the racist crimes are committed by groups (Maung and Mirlees-Black 1994).

The Birmingham Youth Offender Profile does not provide explicit data on violence but can be useful, however, because it delineates problem areas. In 1994 there were 4,319 arrests of young people, but only 2,680 individuals involved because some are arrested more than once. In relation to the totality of Birmingham youth, the highest percentage per age category is that of 15 year olds. Overall 81 per cent are males, 63 per cent are whites, 17 per cent Afro-Caribbean and 15 per cent Asian; 60 per cent of these arrests involve youngster who are less than 16 years old and 16 per cent of those during school hours (Youth Offender Profile 1994). This indicates that such crimes are committed by young people who are playing truant or who have been expelled. Only 7 per cent of crimes are linked to drugs or alcohol. It is also possible to determine the areas which are most affected by arrests of young people. The worst hit are the outer-ring white areas, i.e. deprived working class white areas with more than 3 per cent of the youth population in those areas connected with some crime, followed by some areas of the inner city (between 2.5 and 3 per cent). It is also possible to establish a list of the schools that are most affected (Colin Murphy, West Midlands Police, non-dated).

Institutions Concerned by Violence

The police on the one hand holds the monopoly of legal violence and on the other hand has the responsibility to ensure law and order. Several of the municipality services are more or less directly concerned by the question of violence. The Community Safety Department was created in 1991, two years after a security strategy was developed in Birmingham (Birmingham City Council Community Safety Strategy, estimated 1989) although central government does not tend to give responsibilities to the municipality in this domain (Liddle 1996). Other departments are: Social Services, which is responsible for groups with difficulties such as families, children, adolescents, single mothers, elderly persons, disabled; the Housing Department, which administers social housing; the Leisure and Community Services, Libraries, Community Centres, and on the whole all activities addressing young people; The Local Education Authority and the Race Relations Department. The Probation Service is responsible to central government. Some projects, such as Youth Justice, group several institutions and organisations through a multi-agency approach. Numerous private organisations, NGOs, charities and associations are also concerned. West Midlands Transport which is privatised, the Football Federation which manages teams and stadiums, BRAMU (the Birmingham Racial Attack Monitoring Unit), Crime Concern, NACRO, residents' associations, and the trade unions, particularly the transport workers' and teachers' unions. It is impossible to make an inventory of all the initiatives which deal with potential or effective violence as they are numerous and dispersed. Moreover, such a register does not exist. It is necessary to interview numerous social actors and organisations in order to gather some information about it; I shall thus only quote a few of those projects.

A Police Liaison Committee exists in each area which includes *inter alia* representatives of the police, residents' associations, mosques and temples. Each week the police circulate an internal report on indices of tension in the region. Nationwide, the Association of Chief Police Officers sends to each region a *communiqué* on the hot areas of the summer to come.

'Community Safety' is a Birmingham Local Authority project on security in the community; the Community Safety Project intervenes on two planes. On the one hand it aims to reduce situational factors, for instance, improving lighting in the streets and eliminating subways in the city centre. On the other hand it plans to improve the quality of life and to remedy social causes, for instance it proposes a social education programme, to create jobs or income-generating activities and to reconstitute or consolidate community fabric. Particular attention is granted to young people and to diversion programmes. But women and vulnerable people such as the elderly and victims of racism are addressed through specific projects. In some areas Neighbourhood Watch and Street Watch campaigns have been launched (with the support of the *Daily News*), and Community Development projects (ICP funded) (Birmingham City Council, Community Safety Strategy, estimated 1980). The *Balsall Heathan* (March and April 1996), note that crime accompanied by violence and theft has decreased by 20 per cent since the Street Watch was established. In the Balsall Heath area the Residents' Association is proud of having cleared the area of its prostitutes. Those initiatives particularly target inner-city areas and many outer-ring areas where crime rates are high.

City Challenge (City Regeneration Programme) is a project aiming to regenerate the area of Newtown, Aston. A Community Safety Shop has been installed in a deprived area fraught with problems of thefts, robberies, noise, children in the streets and high child mortality. A police sergeant is responsible for the reduction of crime in the area and for the setting up of Neighbourhood Watches. Most of those involved are young people (15 is the most critical age), several of whom have been expelled from school. A Youth Project was launched to create a football league for children between 12 and 15: 10 managers, six teams, 74 boys, 70 per cent of whom are Bangladeshi and 20 per cent Afro-Caribbean. A Street Wise Project also was set up which gives advice on precautions to take, such as which side of the pavement is safer, which distributes whistles and other safety devices.

The Youth Bureau was launched at the General Assembly of Youth Justice in Birmingham. Its staff aim to help young minors charged with a crime but who do not appear in court to help them not to fall back into new crimes. This is called 'Primary Diversion' (Youth Justice in Birmingham, 1995). The aims of this Bureau are the following: to maintain and increase the diversion rate (i.e. cases which are not caught up in the judiciary system); to reduce people crime and its impact on victims, and to give information on youth crime to a forum bringing together several institutions.

If those young people appear in court, several alternatives to prison are presented in the shape of an appropriate programme which is managed by the Youth Bureau Specified Activity Order and may involve community service or attendance at the centre, for example). More than 80 per cent of those who have benefited from diversion do not relapse within two years, whereas 80 per cent of those who have been jailed commit a new crime within the two years following their release (Enos Houghton, 1996). This organisation functions thanks to collaboration between several organisations: The West Midland Police, Social Services, the LEA, Leisure and Community Services and the Probation Service. The Bureau advises the young people concerned, talks about the reasons why they have committed a crime, discuss his or her problem, and help to resolve them: for instance, finding part-time jobs, obtaining reinstatement in the school or sending the person to another specialised association if it is judged necessary (such as an association that deals with young people and drugs). This initiative entirely relies upon the goodwill of the Police Commissioner in the region, and he can decide to terminate it at any moment. A parallel project exists for young people who are no longer minors and therefore come under the remit of the Probation Service. A project of secondary diversion also exists for those who have been in prison, with the aims of diverting them from new crime and new prison sentences. In Birmingham there are five juvenile justice centres for young people who have been convicted. Those centres are responsible for the supervision and secondary diversion which will sometimes be accompanied by a mentoring project.

Activities for young people aim to decrease the scope of delinquency. Given the importance of young people, community centres where youth workers offer youth activities are central points in deprived areas where unemployment is severe. Some detached projects also exists whereby two youth workers work with young people in the street and other public spaces where they gather (Warstock and Billesley Detached Youth Project 1991, 1992). There are all together 84 youth workers' posts in Birmingham which come under the municipality, with, in addition, numerous projects launched by charities and non-governmental organisations.

There are in addition private initiatives related to security. In Birmingham 49.5 per cent of homes do not possess a car and must use public transport. In public transport, plain clothes police sometimes circulate on a bus on itineraries signalled as the most vulnerable ones. Some buses are provided with cameras and are followed by police cars. In addition, there is a security team employed by Birmingham Transport. Where football is concerned, each stadium has a committee in charge of security which recruits its stewards and trains them.

The Federations (FA), have adopted a preventative strategy developing collaboration with the police.

Appendix II

Sociological Intervention

Interlocutors

Session 1   Closed session
Session 2   Robert Beckford – Black theologian and church leader
Session 3   Ray Griffiths – Regional secretary of Amalgamated Engineers
             and Electrical Union (AEEU)
Session 4   Theresa Stewart – Leader of Birmingham City Council
Session 5   Malcolm Ross – Chairman of the Fordbridge Residents'
             Association
Session 6   Bini Brown – Leader of the African-Caribbean Self-Help
             Organisation. Community Leader and Pan-Africanist
Session 7   Closed session
Session 8   Chris Marsden – Representative for British Petroleum
Session 9   Superintendent Bill Guest – Head of Community Services
             Department
Session 10   John Simmitt – Stand-up comedian, and community arts
             organiser
Session 11   Andrea Reynolds – WPC from Coventry police force
Session 12   Closed session
Session 13   Closed session
Session 14   Closed session – final session

Bibliography

1991 Census Topic Report, *Children and Young People*, Birmingham City Council.

1991 Census Topic Report, *Overview Report*, Birmingham City Council.

1991 Census Topic Reports, *Deprivation and Disadvantage*, Birmingham City Council.

1991 Census Topic Reports, *Ethnic Groups in Birmingham*, Birmingham City Council.

AFFOR (1978), *Talking Blues*, Birmingham: AFFOR.

An address and telephone list for youth organisations in Birmingham: Community Leisure Centres; Department of Leisure and Community Services, Full-time youth and community workers (estimated 1996).

Anderson, B. (1983), *Imagined Communities*, London: Verso.

Anderson, B. and King, R. (1996), Interview, Birmingham 3 April, NUT.

Anthias, F. (1992), *Ethnicity, Class, Gender and Migration. Greek-Cypriots in Britain* Aldershot: Avebury.

Anthias, F. (1998), 'Connecting Ethnicity, "Race", Gender and Class in Ethnic Relations Research', in D. Joly (ed.), *Scapegoats and Social Actors*, Basingstoke: Macmillan.

Anthias, F. and Lloyd, C. (eds) (in press), *Rethinking Antiracism: From theory to practice*, London: Routledge.

Anthias, F. and Yuval-Davis, N. (1992), *Racialized Boundaries. Race, Nation, Gender, Colour and Class and the Anti-racist Struggle*, London: Routledge.

Asad, T. (1990) ,'Ethnography, Literature and Politics: Some readings and uses of Salman Rushdie's *The Satanic Verses*', *Cultural Anthropology*, 5, 3.

Back, L. (1995), *New Ethnicities and Urban Culture. Racisms and Multiculture in Young Lives*, London: UCL Press.

Back, L. (1996), *New Ethnicities and Urban Culture*, London: UCL.

Back, L. and Nayak, A. (eds) (1993), *Invisible Europeans? Black People in the 'New Europe'*, Birmingham: All Faiths for One Race.

Back, L. and Solomos, J. (1993), 'Doing Research, Writing Politics: The dilemmas of political intervention in research on racism', *Economy and Society*, 22, 2.

Ballis Lal, B. (1986), 'The "Chicago School" of American Sociology, Symbolic Interactionism, and Race Relations Theory', in J. Rex and D. Mason (eds), *Theories of Race and Ethnic Relations*, Cambridge: Cambridge University Press, pp. 280–98.

Banton, M. (1967), *Race Relations*, London: Tavistock.

Barth, F. (1969), *Ethnic Groups and Boundaries*, London: Allen and Unwin.

Basch, L., Glick Schiller, N. and Szanton Blanc, C. (1994), *Nations Unbound, Transnational Projects, Post-colonial Predicaments, and Deterritorialised Nation-states*, Langhorne, Pa: Gordon and Breach.

Bauman, G. (1997), 'The Making and Unmaking of Strangers', in P. Werbner and T. Modood (eds), *Debating Cultural Hybridity*, London and New Jersey: Zed Books, pp. 29–46.

Bauman, Z. (1997), 'Dominant and Demotic Discourses of Culture: Their relevance to multi-ethnic alliances', in P. Werbner and T. Modood (eds), *Debating Cultural Hybridity*, London and New Jersey: Zed Books, pp. 193–209.

Benyon, J. and Solomos, J. (eds) (1987), *The Roots of Urban Unrest*, Oxford: Pergamon.

Bhabha, H.K. (1994), *The Location of Culture*, London: Routledge.

Bindman, G. (1994), 'A Racial Violence and Harassment Bill', *New Community*, Vol. 20, No. 3, April, pp. 526–9.

Birmingham City Council (estimated 1989), *Community Safety Strategy*, Birmingham.

Birmingham City Council (1990), Report of Director of Housing to: Housing Management Committee 9 November 1989; General Purposes (Crime Prevention Sub) Committee 17 November 1989; Personnel and Equal Opportunities (Policy and Community Sub) Committee 4 January 1990; An analysis of Racial Harassment Cases on Council Estates.

Birmingham City Council (1992), Report to Divisional Management Team 13 August 1992, Racial Harassment Statistics, January–June 1992.

Birmingham City Council (1996), Report to Housing Management Sub-committee, Joint Race Relations Sub-Committee; Report of the Director of Housing; An analysis of racial harassment on council estates and review of policy and procedures, 15 February 1996, Birmingham.

Birmingham City Council (n.d.), *Make a Difference, All Different, All Equal.*

Birmingham City Council Education Department (1996), *LEA Guidelines Exclusions*, February.

Birmingham City Council Housing Department (1992), Report to Housing Committee 13 February 1992, An Analysis of Racial Harassment Cases on Council Estates.

Birmingham City Council Housing Department (1995), An Analysis of Racial Harassment Cases on Council Estates, Report to Housing Management Sub-Committee 26 January.

Birmingham City Council Housing Department (1995), Race Equality Strategy.

Birmingham City Council Housing Department (n.d.), Key Facts, Race and Housing in Birmingham.

Birmingham City Council Youth Service, Department of Recreation and Community Services, Policy and Curriculum.

Birmingham Leisure (1994), Mirfield Centre Annual Report 1993/94.

Birmingham Partnership Against Racial Harassment.

Birmingham Sports Newsletter for Young People (1996), March.

Birmingham Voice (1996), No. 98, 1 May (from Birmingham City Council).

Birmingham Youth Bureau (1995), *Annual Report (Our First Year)*, 21 July 1994, 25 May.

Björgo, T. and Witte, R. (eds) (1993), *Racist Violence in Europe*, Basingstoke: Macmillan.

Blauner, R.(1969), 'Internal Colonialism and Ghetto Revolt', *Social Problems*, 16, Spring, pp. 393–408.

Blauner, R. (1972), *Racial Oppression in America*, New York: Harper and Row.

Body-Gendrot, S. (1995), 'Urban Violence: A quest for meaning', *New Community*, Vol. 21, No. 4, October.

Bolzman, Claudio (n.d.), *Stages and Modes of Incorporation of Exiles in Switzerland: The example of Chilean refugees.*

Bonacich, E. (1938), 'A Theory of Middleman Minorities', *American Sociological Review*, 38, October, pp. 583–94.

Bonacich, E. (1972), 'A Theory of Ethnic Antagonism: The split labour market', *American Sociological Review.*

Bonnett, A. (1993), *Radicalism, Anti-racism and Representation*, London: Routledge.

Bonnett, A. (1999), *Anti-racism*, London: Routledge.

Bourdieu, P. (1986), 'The Forms of Capital', in J.G. Richardson (ed.), *Handbook of Theory and Research for the Sociology of Education*, New York: Greenwood Press, pp. 241–58.

Bourne, J. (1980), 'Cheerleaders and Ombudsmen: The sociology of race relations in Britain', *Race and Class*, Vol. XXI, Spring, No. 4.

Bowling, B. (1993a), 'Racial Harassment and the Process of Victimisation: Conceptual and methodological implications for the local crime survey', *British Journal of Criminology*, Vol. 33, No. 2, Spring.

Bowling, B. (1993b), *Policing Violent Racism: Policy and practice in an East London locality*, thesis (not published), December.

Bradford Youth Research Team (1987), *Young People in Bradford*, Survey, Department of Applied and Community Studies, Bradford and Ilkley Community College, Bradford.

Brah, A. (1991), 'Difference, Diversity, Differentiation', *International Review of Sociology*, New Series 2, pp. 53–72.

Brah, A. (1996), *Cartographies of Diaspora*, London: Routledge.

Brown, C. (1984), *Black and White Britain: The third PSI Survey*, London: Heinemann.

Brown, C. (1986), *Racial Discrimination: 17 years after the act*, London: PSI.

BRUM, Birmingham City Council Community Safety Cautioning, 23 September 1994.

Burlet, S. and Reid, H. (1995), 'Cooperation and Conflict: The South Asian diaspora after Ayodhya', *New Community*, Vol. 21, No. 4, October.

Caglar, A.S. (1997), 'Hyphenated Identities and the Limits of "Culture"', in T. Modood and P. Werbner (eds), *The Politics of Multiculturalism in the New Europe*, London and New York: Zed Books, pp. 169–86.

Campani, G., Catani, M. and Pallida, S. (1987), 'Italian Immigrant Associations in France', in J. Rex, D. Joly and C. Wilpert (eds), *Immigrant Associations in Europe*, Aldershot: Gower.

Candappa, M. and Joly, D. (1994), *Local Authorities, Ethnic Minorities and 'Pluralist' Integration*, Coventry: CRER.

Candappa, M. and Joly, D. (1994), *Local Authorities, Ethnic Minorities and 'Pluralist Integration'*, Monographs in Ethnic Relations No. 7, CRER, University of Warwick.

Carby, H. (1982), 'White Woman Listen! Black Feminism and the Boundaries of Sisterhood', in CCCS, *The Empire Strikes Back: Race and Racism in '70s Britain*, London: Hutchinson.

Carby, H.V. (1982), 'Schooling in Babylon', in CCCS, *The Empire Strikes Back: Race and racism in '70s Britain*, Centre for Contemporary Cultural Studies, London: Hutchinson.

Carby, H.V. (1987), *Reconstructing Womanhood*, Oxford: Oxford University Press.

Carey-Wood, J. (1997), *Meeting Refugees' Needs in Britain: The role of refugee specific initiative*, London: Home Office Research and Statistics Directorate.

CARF (1998), 'Is Labour Failing Black Children?', *CARF*, 45, September.

Castles, S. and Kosack, G. (1973), *Immigrant Workers and Class Structure in Western Europe*, Oxford: OUP/IRR.

Centre for Contemporary Cultural Studies (1982), *The Empire Strikes Back: Race and racism in '70s Britain*, London: Hutchinson.

Childs, P. and Williams, P. (1997), *An Introduction to Post-Colonial Theory*, London: Harvester Wheatsheaf.

Chinn, C. (1994), *Birmingham the Great Working City*, Birmingham City Council.

Chinn, C. (1996), telephone interview, Birmingham, 15 March.

City of Birmingham (n.d.), *Social Crime Prevention: A new approach*, Birmingham.

Clifford, J. (1992), 'Travelling Cultures', in L. Grossberg et al. (eds), *Cultural Studies*, London: Routledge.

Clifford, J. (1994), 'Diasporas', *Cultural Anthropology*, 9 (3) pp. 302–38.

Coard, B. (1971), *How the West Indian Child is made Educationally Subnormal in the British School System*, London: New Beacon Books.

Cohen, P. (1992), '"It's Racism What Dunnit": Hidden narratives in theories of racism', in J. Donald and A. Rattansi (eds), *'Race', Culture and Difference*, London: Sage.

Cohen, P. (1993), *Home Rules: Some reflections on racism and nationalism in everyday life*, London: University of East London.

Cohen, P. (1997), *Rethinking the youth question: education, labour and cultural studies*, Basingstoke: Macmillan.

Coleman, D. (1985), 'Ethnic Intermarriage in Great Britain', *Population Trends*, No. 40.

Coleman, D. and Salt, J. (eds) (1996), *Ethnicity in the 1991 Census, Vol. 1: Demographic characteristics of the ethnic minority populations*, London: HMSO.

Commission for Racial Equality (1981), *Submission under Part II of Lord Scarman's Inquiry into the Brixton Disorder (the Underlying Causes)*, June, London: CRE.

Commission for Racial Equality (1984a), *Race and Council Housing in Hackney*, London: CRE.

Commission for Racial Equality (1984b), *Race and Housing in Liverpool: A research report*, London: CRE.

Commission for Racial Equality (1984c), *Immigration Control Procedures*, London: CRE.

Commission for Racial Equality (1985), *Ethnic Minorities in Britain: Statistical information on the pattern of settlement*, London: CRE.

Commission for Racial Equality (1985), *Review of the Race Relations Act 1976: Proposals for change*, London: CRE.

Commission for Racial Equality (1986), *Black Teachers, the Challenge of Increasing the Supply*, CRE: London.

Commission for Racial Equality (1988), *St George's Hospital Medical School*, London: CRE.

Commission for Racial Equality (1992), *Second Review of the Race Relations Act*, London: CRE.

Commission for Racial Equality (1997), *The Irish in Britain*, London: CRE.

Commission on British Muslims and Islamophobia (1997), *Islamophobia: A challenge for us all: summary*, Runnymede Trust.

Corrigan, Philip (1989), 'Why Muslims are Treated Differently. A Commentary on the So-called "Rushdie Affair" and Ethnic Nationalism', Open Seminars, CRER, 29 November, unpublished.

Couper, K. (1990), 'Petit Lexique Britannique en Matière d'Hommes et Migrations', *Hommes et Migrations*, No. 1137, November.

CRE (1987), *Living in Terror*, London: CRE.

CRE (1988), *Learning in Terror*, London: CRE.

Crime Concern (1992), *Annual Review.*

Cross, M., Cox, B., Johnson, M. (1988), 'Black Welfare and Local Government, Section 11 and Social Services Department', CRER, University of Warwick, *Policy Papers*, No. 12.

Cross, M., Cox, B., Johnson, M. (1988), *Poor Black Welfare: Ethnic Minorities, Social Services and Marginal Money*, CRER, University of Warwick, mimeo, Coventry.

Daniel, W.W. (1968), *Racial Discrimination in England*, London: PEP/Penguin.

de Rudder, V., Taboada, I. and Vourc'h, F. (1994), 'Immigrant Participation and Mobilisation and Integration Strategies in France: A typology', in J. Rex and B. Drury (eds), *Ethnic Mobilisation in a Multi-cultural Europe*, Aldershot: Avebury, pp. 116–22.

Deakin, N. (1970), *Colour, Citizenship and British Society*, London: Panther.

Dear, G. (1985), *Report of the Chief Constable West Midlands Police Handsworth/ Lozells – September 1985.*

Department for Education (1993), *Exclusions: A discussion paper.*

Department for Education and Employment (2000) Statistics of Education: Permanent Exclusions from Maintained Schools in England, Bulletin 10/00, November.

Department of the Environment (1989), *Tackling Racial Violence and Harassment in Local Authority Housing*, London: HMSO.

Drury, B. (1995), 'Ethnic Mobilisation: Some theoretical considerations', in J. Rex and B. Drury (eds), *Ethnic Mobilisation in a Multi-cultural Europe*, Aldershot: Avebury, pp. 13–22.

Dubet, F. (1998), *La Méthode* (unpublished, Paris CADIS).

Dubet, F. (1999), 'Où en est la Méthode de l'Intervention Sociologique', CADIS Seminar Paris: 6 January.

Dubet, F. and Wieviorka, M. (1996), 'Touraine and the Method of Sociological Intervention', in J. Clark and M. Diani (eds), *Alain Touraine*, London: Falmer, pp. 55–75.

Duffield, M. (1988), *Black Radicalism and the Politics of De-Industrialisation: 'The Hidden History of Indian Foundry Workers'*, Avebury, Aldershot.

Dummett, A. (1973), *A Portrait of English Racism*, London: Penguin.

Dummett, A. and Nicol, A. (1990), *Subjects, Citizens, Aliens and Others: Nationality and immigration law*, London: Weidenfeld and Nicolson.

Duncan, C. (1987), 'Understanding Multicultural/Anti-Racist Education for Practice', in T.S. Chivers (ed.), *Race and Culture in Education*, NFER-Nelson: Berkshire.

Dunning, E.G., Murphy, P. and Williams, J. (1982), *Working Class Social Bonding and the Sociogenesis of Football Hooliganism*, a report to the Social Science Research Council.

Dunning, E.G., Murphy, P. and Williams, J. (1986), 'Spectator Violence at Football Matches: Towards a sociological explanation', *British Journal of Sociology*, No.2, June.

Dunning, E.G., Murphy, P. and Williams, J. (1986), *Spectator Violence Associated with Football Matches: A state of the art review*, paper prepared for the Sports Council on behalf of the Council of Europe.

Dunning, E.G., Murphy, P. and Williams, J. (1988), *The Roots of Football Hooliganism*, Routledge and Kegan Paul.

Dunning, E.G., Murphy, P., Williams, J. and Maguire, J. (1984), 'Football Hooliganism in Britain before the First World War', *International Review of the Sociology of Sport*, Vol. 19, No. 3–4.

Dyer, R. (1988), 'White', *Screen*, 29, 4, pp. 44–5.

Education Service Advisory Committee (1990), *Violence to Staff in the Education Sector*, London: HMSO.

Eisenstadt (1954), *The Absorption of Immigrants*, Routledge and Kegan Paul.

Eriksen, T.H. (1993), *Ethnicity and Nationalism*, London: Pluto.

Faist, T. (1999), 'Developing Transnational Social Spaces: The Turkish-German example', in L. Pries (ed.), *Migration and Transnational Social Spaces*, Tyne and Wear: Athenaeum Press, pp. 36–73.

Faist, T. (2000), 'Transnationalisation in International Migration: Implications for the study of citizenship and culture', *Ethnic and Racial Studies*, Vol. 23, No. 2, March.

Fanon, F. (1975), *Pour la Révolution Africaine*, Paris: Maspéro.

Fekete, L. and Webber, F. (1994), *Inside Racist Europe*, London: Institute of Race Relations.

Ford, G. (1990), *Report on the Findings of the Committee of Inquiry into Racism and Xenophobia*, Strasbourg: European Parliament.

Ford, G. (1992), *Europe. The Rise of Racism and Xenophobia*, London: Pluto.

Friedman, Jonathan (1997), 'Global Crises, the Struggle for Cultural Identity and Intellectual Porkbarrelling: Cosmopolitans versus locals, ethnics and nationals in an era of de-hegemonisation', in P. Werbner and T. Modood (eds), *Debating Cultural Hybridity*, London and New Jersey: Zed Books, pp. 58–70.

Furnival, J. (1939), *Netherlands India*, Cambridge: Cambridge University Press.

Geddes, M. (1995), 'Immigration and Ethnic Minorities and the European Union's Democratic Deficit', *Journal of Common Market Studies*, Vol. 33, No. 2, pp. 197–217.

Geertz, C. (1963), *Old Societies and New States – The Quest for Modernity in Asia and Africa*, Glencoe Illinois: Free Press.

Gibson, A. (1980), *Pregnancy Among Unmarried West Indian Teenagers*, Centre for Caribbean Studies, London.

Gilbourne, D. (1993), *Racial Violence*, London: Institute of Education.

Gilroy, P. (1982), 'Police and Thieves', in CCCS, *The Empire Strikes Back: Race and racism in '70s Britain*, London: Centre for Contemporary Cultural Studies, Hutchinson.

Gilroy, P. (1982), 'Steppin' out of Babylon – Race, Class and Autonomy', in CCCS, *The Empire Strikes Back: Race and racism in '70s Britain*, Centre for Contemporary Cultural Studies, Hutchinson.

Gilroy, P. (1986), *There Ain't no Black in the Union Jack*, London: Hutchinson.

Gilroy, P. (1993a), *The Black Atlantic*, London: Verso.

Gilroy, P. (1993b), *Small Acts. Thoughts on the Politics of Black Cultures*, London: Serpent's Tail.

Glazer, N. and Moynihan, D. (1970), *Beyond the Melting Pot*, MIT Press.

Glazer, N. and Moynihan, D. (eds) (1975), *Ethnicity: Theory and experience*, Cambridge, Mass.: Harvard University Press.

Gold, S.J. (1992), *Refugee Communities*, London: Sage.

Goldring, Luin (1999), 'Power and Status in Transnational Social Spaces', in L. Pries (ed.), *Migration and Transnational Social Spaces*, Tyne and Wear: Athenaeum Press, pp. 162–87.

Good Practice (1995), 'Neighbour Nuisance: Ending the nightmare', Issue 3, December.

Goodwin-Gill, G. (1983), *The Refugee in International Law*, Oxford: Clarendon Press.

Gordon, M.M. (1978), *Human Nature, Class and Ethnicity*, Oxford: Oxford University Press.

Gordon, P. (1985), *Policing Immigration. Britain's Internal Controls*, London: Pluto.

Gordon, P. (1986), *Racial Violence and Harassment*, London: Runnymede Trust.

Goulbourne, H. (1991), *Ethnicity and Nationalism in Post-Imperial Britain*, Cambridge University Press: Cambridge.

Goulbourne, H. and Joly, D. (1989) 'Religion and Asian and Caribbean Minorities', *Contemporary European Affairs*, No. 4, Vol. 2, Politics and Religion, pp. 77–98.

Govaert, S. (1995), 'Flander's Radical Nationalism: How and why the *Vlaams Blok* ascended', *New Community*, Vol. 21, No. 4, October.

Greening, J. (1996), Interview, Birmingham, 3 May, West Midlands Police.

Grewal, M.L. (1985), *The Handsworth Disturbances*, Department of Sociology, University of Warwick, MA, mimeo.

Griffiths, M. and Troyna, B. (1995), 'Anti-racism, Culture and Social Justice in Education', in D. Tattum (ed.), *Disruptive Pupil: Understanding and managing bullying*, Heinemann.

Guest, T. (1995), A Study of Racial Violence and Harassment in the West Midlands with an Examination of the Police Response, Birmingham.

Guest, T. (1996), Interview, Birmingham, 2 April, West Midlands Police.

Guest, T. (1996), Interview, Birmingham, 3 May, West Midlands Police.

Gurnah, A. (1987), 'Gatekeepers and Caretakers: Swann, Scarman and the social policy of containment', in B. Troyna (ed.), *Racial Equality in Education*, London: Tavistock.

Hall, S. (1980), 'Race, Articulation and Societies Structured in Dominance', in *UNESCO, Sociological Theories: Race and colonialism*, Paris: UNESCO.

Hall, S. (1990), 'Cultural Identity and Diaspora', in J. Rutherford (ed.), *Identity: Community, culture, difference*, London: Lawrence and Wishart.

Hall, S. (1992), 'The New Ethnicities', in J. Donald and A. Rattansi (eds), *'Race', Culture and Difference*, London: Sage.

Hall, S. et al. (1978), *Policing the Crisis: Mugging, the state and law and order*, London: Macmillan.

Hall, S. and du Gay (1996), *Questions of Cultural Identity*, London: Sage.

Hall, S. and Jacques, M. (eds) (1989), *New Times: The changing face of politics in the 1990s*, London: Lawrence and Wishart.

Harvey, D. (1996), *Justice, Nature and the Geography of Difference*, Oxford: Blackwell.

Hathaway, J.C. (1984), 'The Evolution of Refugee Status in International Law: 1920–1950', 33, *ICLQ*, pp. 348–80.

Herrera, P. and Joly, D. (1989), Chronology of the Salman Rushdie Affair, Birmingham: unpublished.

Hickman, M. and Walter, B. (1997), 'Discrimination and the Irish community in Britain: A report of research undertaken for the CRE', London: Commission for Racial Equality.

Hill, J. (1996), Interview, Birmingham, 1 May, LEA.

Hily, M.-A. and Poinard, M. (1987), 'Portuguese Associations in France', in J. Rex, D. Joly and C. Wilpert (eds), *Immigrant Associations in Europe*, Aldershot: Gower.

Hiro, D. (1971), *Black British, White British*, London: Monthly Review Press.

Hirst, P. and Thompson, G. (1996), *Globalisation in Question*, Cambridge: Polity Press.

Hobsbawm, E.J. (1973), *Revolutionaries: Contemporary essays*, London: Weidenfeld and Nicolson.

Hobsbawm, E.J. (1994), *The Age of Empire*, London: Abacus.

Hobsbawm, E.J. (1994), *Age of Extremes: The short twentieth century, 1914–1991*, London: Michael Joseph.

Holland, B. (1995), '"Kicking Racism out of Football": An assessment of racial harassment in and around football grounds', *New Community*, Vol. 21, No. 4, October.

Holland, M. (1996), Interview, Birmingham, 23 May, LEA.

Home Office (1988), *A Scrutiny of Grants Under Section 11 of the Local Government Act 1966*, Final Report, mimeo, December.

Home Office (1989), *The Response to Racial Attacks and Harassment: Guidance for the statutory agencies*, Report of the inter-departmental racial attacks group, London.

Home Office (1991), *The Response to Racial Attacks: Sustaining the momentum*, London.

Home Office (1994), *The Cautioning of Offenders*, Circular 18/1994, 14 March.

Houghton, E. (1996), Interview, Birmingham, 1 April, Juvenile Justice.

How, S. (1996), Interview, Birmingham, 18 April, Community Safety Department.

Hutton, W. (1996), *The State We're In*, London: Vintage.

Institute of Race Relations (1987), *Policing Against Black People*, London: IRR.

Inter-Departmental Racial Attacks Group (1991), *The Response to Racial Attacks: Sustaining the momentum*, London: HMSO.

James, S. and Busia, A. (eds) (1993), *Theorising Black Feminisms*, London: Routledge.

James, W. and Harris, C. (1993), *Inside Babylon: The Caribbean diaspora in Britain*, London: Verso.

Jenkins, J.C. (1983), 'Resource Mobilisation Theory and the Study of Social Movements', *Annual Review of Sociology*, pp. 527–53.

Jenkins, R. (1986), 'Social Anthropological Models of Inter-ethnic Relations', in J. Rex and D. Mason (eds), *Theories of Race and Ethnic Relations*, Cambridge: Cambridge University Press, pp. 170–86.

Jenkins, R. (1997), *Rethinking Ethnicity*, London: Sage.

Jenkins, R. and Solomos, J. (1987), *Racism and Equal Opportunity Policies in the 1980s*, Cambridge: Cambridge University Press.

Johnson, M., Cross, M., Parker, R. (1981), *Ethnic Minorities and the Inner City*, paper given at the Institute of British Geographers, Annual Conference.

Joint Commission Against Racialism (1981), *Racial Violence in Britain 1980*, paper presented to the Home Secretary, 4 February, London.

Joly, D. (1987), 'Associations amongst the Pakistani Population in Britain', in J. Rex, D. Joly and C. Wilpert (eds), *Immigrant Associations in Europe*, Aldershot: Gower, pp. 62–85.

Joly, D. (1987), 'Mosques and Islam as a Minority Religion', Committee on the Comparative Study of Muslim Societies, Conference on Muslims under Non-Muslim Rule, Delhi, 14–19 December.

Joly, D. (1988), 'Immigration, Citoyenneté et Pouvoir Local: les Pakistanais à Birmingham', in R. Leveau and G. Kepel (eds), *Les Musulmans dans la Société Français*, Paris: PUF.

Joly, D. (1988), 'Making a Place for Islam in British Society: Muslims in Birmingham', in T. Gerholm and Y.G. Litman (eds), *The New Islamic Presence in Western Europe*, London: Mansell.

Joly, D. (1989), 'Ethnic Minorities and Education: The interaction between Muslims and schools in Birmingham', in *Muslims in Europe Research Papers*, No. 41, Selly Oak Colleges, Birmingham March.

Joly, D. (1989), 'Le Droit d'Asile dans la Communauté Européenne', *International Journal of Refugee Law*, Vol. 1, No. 3, Oxford.

Joly, D. (1991), 'La Jeunesse Pakistanaise Musulmane de Birmingham', *Les Temps Modernes*, No. 6, July–August.

Joly, D. (1992), 'Minorités Ethniques et Risques de Ségrégation', in D. Lapeyronnie (ed.), *Immigrés en Europe, Politiques locales d'intégration*, Documentation Française, Paris, pp. 111–37.

Joly, D. (1995), *Britannia's Crescent: Making a place for Muslims in British society*, Aldershot: Ashgate.

Joly, D. (1996), *Haven or Hell: Asylum policies and refugees in Europe*, Oxford, Macmillan.

Joly, D. (1996), The context for a new research programme, Coventry, unpublished.

Joly, D. (1998), 'Ethnicité et Violence chez les /jeunes Antillais: ///une intervention sociologique à Birmingham', *Cahiers Internationaux de Sociologie*, Vol. CV.

Joly, D. (1998), *Scapegoats or Social Actors: The exclusion and integration of minorities in Western and Eastern Europe*, Basingstoke: Macmillan.

Joly, D. (1999), 'A New Asylum Regime in Europe', in F. Nicholson and P. Twomey (eds), *Refugee Rights and Realities*, Cambridge: Cambridge University Press.

Joly, D. and Cohen, R. (eds) (1989), *Reluctant Host: Europe and its refugees*, Aldershot: Gower Press.

Joly, D. with Nettleton, C. and Poulton, H. (1992), *Refugees: Asylum in Europe?*, London: MRG.

Jones, P. (1982), *Vietnamese Refugees: A study of their reception and resettlement in the United Kingdom*, Research and Planning Unit, Paper 13, London: Home Office.

Josephides, S. (1989), *Towards a History of the Indian Workers' Association*, CRER: University of Warwick.

Juss, S. (1993), *Immigration, Nationality and Citizenship*, with a foreword by Stephen Sedley, London: Mansell.

Karn, V. (ed.) (1997), *Ethnicity in the 1991 Census Vol. 4: Employment, education and housing among the ethnic minority populations of Britain*, London: The Stationery Office, pp. 29–66.

Kay, D. (1987), *Chileans in Exile: Private struggles, public lives*, London: Macmillan.

Kay, D. and Miles, R. (1992), *Refugees or Migrant Workers? European Volunteer Workers in Britain 1946–1951*, London: Routledge.

Keane, J. (1996), *Reflections on Violence*, London: Verso.

Keith, M. (1995), 'Making the Street Visible: Placing racial violence in context', *New Community*, Vol. 21, No. 4, October.

Keith, M. and Pile, S. (eds) (1993), *Place and the Politics of Identity*, London: Routledge.

Kelly, L. and Joly, D. (1999), *Refugees' reception and Settlement in Britain*, Coventry, A report for the Joseph Rowntree Foundation.

Kettle, M. and Hodges, L. (1982), *Uprising*, London: Pan Books.

Khan, S.V. (1977), 'The Pakistanis: Mirpuri villagers at home and in Bradford', in J. Watson (ed.), *Between Two Cultures*, Oxford: Basil Blackwell, pp. 57–89.

King, J. (1994), *Three Asian Associations in Britain*, Monograph in Ethnic Relations No. 8, CRER, University of Warwick, Coventry.

Koffman, E. (1998), 'Female Birds of Passage a Decade Later. Gender and Immigration in the European Union', *International Migration Review*.

Kunz, E.F. (1973), 'The Refugee in Flight: Kinetic models and forms of displacement', *International Migration Review*, Vol. 7, No.2, pp. 125–46.

Kunz, E.F. (1981), 'Exile and Resettlement: Refugee theory', *International Migration Review*, Vol. 15 (1–2), pp. 42–51.

Lapeyronnie, D. (1990), *Les Politiques Locales d'Intégration des Minorités Immigrées en Europe et aux Etats Unis*, Paris: ADRI.

Lapeyronnie, D. (1993), *L'Individu et les Minorités: la France et la Grande-Bretagne face à leurs immigrés*, PUF, Paris.

Lapeyronnie, D., Forbes, M., Couper, K. and Joly, D. (1990), *L'Intégration des Minorités Immigrées: Etude comparative: France: Grande Bretagne*, Paris: ADRI.

Lawrence, E. (1982), 'In the Abundance of Water the Fool is Thirsty: Sociology and black "pathology"', in CCCS, *The Empire Strikes Back: Race and racism in '70s Britain*, London: Centre for Contemporary Cultural Studies, Hutchinson.

Lawrence, E. (1982) 'Just Plain Common Sense: The "roots" of racism', in CCCS, *The Empire Strikes Back: Race and racism in '70s Britain*, London: Centre for Contemporary Cultural Studies, Hutchinson.

Layton-Henry, Z. (1990), *The Political Rights of Migrant Workers in Western Europe*, London: Sage.

Layton-Henry, Z. (1992), *The Politics of Immigration: Immigration, 'race' and 'race relations' in Britain since 1945*, Oxford: Blackwells.

LEA exclusion guideline (1996a), Birmingham.

LEA guideline on the care, welfare and protection of pupil and staff Birmingham, (1996b) (April 1996).

Leveau, R. and Kepel, G. (eds) (1988), *Les Musulmans dans la Societé Française*, Paris: PUF.

Levitas, R. (1996), 'The Concept of Social Exclusion and the New Durkheimian Hegemony', *Critical Social Policy*, 16(46), pp. 5–20.

Liddle, M. (1996), Interview, Birmingham, 24 April.

Liddle, M. (forthcoming), *Community Safety and the City.*

Liddle, M. and Gelsthorpe, L. (1994), *Inter-agency Crime Prevention: Organising local delivery*, Police Research Group, Crime Prevention Unit Series, Paper 52.

Liddle, M. and Gelsthorpe, L. (1994), *Inter-agency Crime Prevention: Further issues*, Police Research Group, Supplementary Paper to CPU Series Paper No. 52 and 53, London: Home Office Police Department.

Liddle, M. and Gelsthorpe, L. (1994), *Crime Prevention and Inter-agency Co-operation*, Police Research Group, Crime Prevention Unit Series Paper 53, London: Home Office Police Department.

Lloyd, C. (1995), *The Irish Community in Britain: Discrimination, disadvantage, and racism. An annotated bibliography*, London: University of North London Press.

Lloyd, C. (1996), 'Antiracist Strategies: National identity and French antiracist discourses and movements', in T. Ranger et al. (eds), *Culture, Identity and Politics: Ethnic Minorities in Britain*, Aldershot: Avebury.

Lloyd, C. (1998a), *Discourses of Antiracism in France*, Aldershot: Ashgate.

Lloyd, C. (2000), 'Genre, Migration et Ethnicité: Perspectives feministes en Grande Bretagne', Cahren du Cedref No. 7, Université de Paris, 7 Jussien.

Lock, S. (1998), 'Is there a New Deal for Black Youth?', *CARF*, 43, April/May.

Lowe, J. (1996), Interview, Birmingham, 25 May, Leisure and Community Services.

Macdonald, I. et al. (1989), *Murder in the Playground, the Burnage Report*, London: Longsight Press.

Macpherson of Cluny, Sir W. (1999), *The Stephen Lawrence Inquiry*, London: HMSO.

MaMung, E. (1994), 'Groundlessness and Utopia: The Chinese diaspora and territory', paper at international conference *The Last Half-century of Chinese Overseas (1945–1994)*, 19–21 December 1994, University of Hong Kong, Hong Kong.

Manchester Education Committee (1986), *Triangular Minds, Black Youth on Identity*, Manchester: Central Manchester Caribbean Project.

Marshall, T.H. and Bottomore, T. (1992), *Citizenship and Social Class*, London: Pluto.

Marx, K. (1969), *Le 18 Brumaire de Louis Bonaparte*, Paris: Editions Sociales.

Marx, K. (1973), *Surveys from Exile*, edited and introduced by David Fernbach, Harmondsworth: Penguin Books.

Massey, D. et al. (1993), 'Theories of International Migration: A review and appraisal', *Population and Development Review*, Vol. 19, pp. 431–66.

Maung, N.A. and Mirlees-Black, C. (1994), *Racially Motivated Crime: A British crime survey analysis*, Research and Planning Unit Paper 82, London: Home Office.

Melander, G. (1987), *The Two Refugee Definitions*, Report No. 4, Raoul Wallenberg Institute, Lund, pp. 9–22.

Memmi, A. (1972), *Portrait du Colonisé*, Montréal: L'Etincelle.

Merriman, N. (ed.) (1993), *The Peopling of London. Fifteen Thousand Years of Settlement from Overseas*, London: Museum of London.

Miles, R. (1984), 'The Riots of 1958: The ideological construction of "race relations" as a political issue in Britain', *Immigrants and Minorities*, 3(3), pp. 252–75.

Miles, R. (1989), *Racism*, London: Routledge.

Miles, R. (1993), *Racism after 'Race Relations'*, London: Routledge.

Miles, R. and Thranhardt, D. (1995), *Migration and European Integration. The Dynamics of Inclusion and Exclusion*, London: Pinter.

Miller, J. (2000) Profiling Populations Available for Stops and Searches, Police Research Series Paper 131 (London: Home Office).

Modood, T, (1992), *Not Easy being British: Colour, culture and citizenship*, London: Runnymede Trust/Trentham.

Modood, T. (1994), *Ethnic Minorities and Higher Education: Why are there differential rates of entry?*, London: PSI.

Modood, T. (1994), *Racial Equality: Colour, culture and justice*, London: IPPR.

Modood, T. (1997), *Church, State and Religious Minorities*, London: PSI.

Modood, T. (1997a), *Ethnic Minorities in Britain: Diversity and disadvantage*, London: PSI.

Modood, T. et al. (1994), *Changing Ethnic Identities*, London: PSI.

Modood, T., Berthoud, R., Lakey, J., Nazroo, J., Smith, P., Virdee, S. and Beison, S. (1997), *Ethnic Minorities in Britain: Diversity and Disadvantage* (London: PSI).

Modood, T. and Metcalf, H. (1996), *Asian Self-employment: The interaction of culture and economics in England*, London: PSI.

Modood, T. and Werbner, P. (1997), *The Politics of Multiculuralism in the New Europe*, London: Zed.

Moore, R. (1975), *Racism and Black Resistance*, London: Pluto.

Morris, L. (1994), *Dangerous Classes: The underclass and social citizenship*, London: Routledge.

Mulgrew, N. (1996), Interview Birmingham, 28 April, Community Safety Shop, Newtown.

Mullard, C. (1982), 'Multiracial Education in Britain, from Assimilation to Cultural Pluralism', in J. Tierney (ed.), *Race, Migration and Schooling*, London: Holt Rinehart and Winston.

Municipal Publications (1985), *The Municipal Year Book*, London.

Murphy, C., West Midlands Police (n.d.), Birmingham Juvenile Offender Profile 1991, Birmingham, Community Services Dept.

Murphy, P. et al. (1990), *Football on Trial*, London: Routledge.

Myrdal, G. (1944), *An American Dilemma*, New York: Harper Bros.

Myrdal, G. (1964), *Challenge to Affluence*, London: Macmillan.

NACRO (1989), *Diverting Juvenile Offenders from Prosecution*, Juvenile Crime Committee Policy Paper 2, September, London.

NACRO (1992), *Diverting Young Offenders from Prosecution*, Young Offenders Committee Policy Paper 2.

National Union of Teachers (1992), *NUT Survey on Pupil Exclusions: Information from LEAs*, London: NUT.

NIDR News (1994), May–June, National Institute for Dispute Resolution.

Nielsen, J. (1999), *Towards a European Islam*, Basingstoke: Macmillan.

Nielsen, J.-S. (1986), 'A Survey of British Local Authority Response to Muslim Needs', Centre for the Study of Islam and Christian Muslim Relations, *Research Papers Muslims in Europe*, No. 30–31, Birmingham, June–September.

Noor, N.S. and Khalsa, S.S. (1977–78), *Education Needs of Asian Children in the Context of Multiracial Education in Wolverhampton*, a survey of parents' views and attitudes, IWA (GB), Wolverhampton.

NUT (1981), *Combating Racialism in Schools*, a union policy statement: guidance for members, October.

Oakley, R. (1992), *Report on Racial Violence and Harassment in Europe*, Strasbourg: Council of Europe.

Office of Population Censuses and Surveys (OPCS) (1982), *1981 Census – Country of British, Great Britain*, HMSO, London.

Office of Population Censuses and Surveys (OPCS) (1988), *Labour Force Survey 1986*, Series No. 6, HMSO, London.

Office of Population Censuses and Surveys (OPCS) (1989), *Labour Force Survey 1987*, Series No. 7, HMSO, London.

Office of Population Censuses and Surveys (1993), *1991 Census: Ethnic group and country of birth, Great Britain*, HMSO, London.

Olzak, S. and Nagel, Y. (eds) (1986), *Competitive Ethnic Relations*, London: Academic Press.

Owen, D. (1993), 'Country of Birth: Settlement patterns', National Ethnic Minority Data Archive 1991 Census Statistical Paper No. 5, Centre for Research in Ethnic Relations, University of Warwick.

Owen, D. (1997), 'Labour Force Participation Rates, Self-employment and Unemployment', in V. Karn (ed.), *Ethnicity in the 1991 Census Vol. 4: Employment, education and housing among the ethnic minority populations of Britain*, London: The Stationery Officer, pp. 29–66.

Owen, D., Green, A.E., Pitcher, J. and Maguire, M. (2000), 'Minority Ethnic Participation and Achievements in Education, Training and the Labour Market', *DfEE Research Report* 225 (Nottingham: DfEE).

Parekh, B. (1994), *Racial Violence: A Separate Offence? A Discussion Paper*, The All-Party Parliamentary Group on Race and Community, Houses of Parliament, Session 1993/94, London: A Charta Mede Associate Company.

Parffrey, V. (1994), 'Exclusion: Failed children or systems failure?', *School Organisation*, 14, 2, pp. 107–120.

Park, R.E. (1950), *Race and Culture*, Glencoe Illinois: The Free Press.

Parmar, P. (1982), 'Gender, Race and Class: Asian women in resistance', in CCCS *The Empire Strikes Back: Race and racism in '70s Britain*, Centre for Contemporary Cultural Studies, Hutchinson.

Patterson, S. (1968), *Dark Strangers*, London: Penguin.

Peach, C. (ed.) (1996), *Ethnicity in the 1991 Census Vol. 2: The ethnic minority populations of Great Britain*, London: HMSO.

Pearson, G. (1983), *Hooligan*, London: Macmillan.

Petersen, W. (1958), 'A General Typology of Migration', *American Sociological Review*, 23(3) pp. 256–66.

Phizacklea, A. (ed.) (1983), *One-way Ticket*, London: Routledge.

Phizacklea, A. (1995), *Homeworking Women*, London: Sage.

Plant, R. (1988), *Citizenship, Rights and Socialism*, London: Fabian Society.

Platt, L. and Noble, M. (1999) *Race, Place and Poverty: Ethnic groups and low income distributions* (York: York Publishing Services).

Policy Studies Institute (PSI) (1991), *Racial Justice at Work*, PSI.

Population Trends (1986), 'Ethnic Minority Populations in Great Britain', No. 46, Winter.

Pries, L. (1999), *Migration and Transnational Social Spaces*, Aldershot: Ashgate.

Pries, L. (ed.) (1999), 'New Migration in Transnational Spaces', in *Migration and Transnational Social Spaces*, Tyne and Wear: Athenaeum Press, pp. 1–36.

Public Authorities Directory (1989), LGC Communications, London.

Ratcliffe, P. (ed.) (1996), *Ethnicity in the 1991 Census Vol. 3: Social geography and ethnicity in Britain: geographical spread, spatial concentration and internal migration*, London: HMSO.

Rees, G. (1996), Interview, Birmingham, 3 May, West Midlands Police.

Report of the Leisure Services Committee (n.d.).

Review Panel (1986), *A Different Reality: An account of Black people's experiences and their grievances before and after the Handsworth rebellion of September 1985*, February.

Rex, J. (1961), *Key Problems of Sociological Theory*, London: Routledge and Kegan Paul.

Rex, J. (1970), 'The Concept of Race in Sociological Theory', in S. Zubaida (ed.), *Race and Racialism*, London: Tavistock.

Rex, J. (1973), *Race, Colonialism and the City*, London: Routledge and Kegan Paul.

Rex, J. (1979), 'Black Militancy and Class Conflict', in R. Miles and A. Phizacklea, (eds), *Racism and Political Section in Britain*, London: Routledge.

Rex, J. (1986), *Race and Ethnicity*, Milton Keynes: Open University Press.

Rex, J. (1986), *The Concept of a Multi-cultural Society*, Occasional Papers, CRER, University of Warwick.

Rex, J. (1988), *The Ghetto and the Underclass*, Aldershot: Avebury, Gower.

Rex, J. (1989) 'Equality of Opportunity, Multiculturalism, Anti-racism and "Education for All"', in G. Vermah (ed.), *Education for All: a landmark in pluralism*, Falmer: London.

Rex, J. (1990), 'The Reception of Immigrants in Great-Britain', paper delivered at Turin conference, January.

Rex, J. (1992), 'Race and Ethnicity in Europe', in J. Bailey (ed.), *Social Europe*, London: Longmans.

Rex, J. (1996), *Ethnic Minorities in the Modem Nation State: Working papers in the theory of multiculturalism and political integration in European cities*, Basingstoke: Macmillan.

Rex, J. (1996), 'Multiculturalism and Political Integration in European Cities', special issue of *Innovation*, Vol. 9, No. 1, Abingdon: Carfax.

Rex, J. (1997), 'Multiculturalism and Political Integration in European Cities', paper to Forum International des Sciences Humaines Cultural Difference, Racism and Democracy, Paris, 18–20 September.

Rex, John (1995), 'Ethnic Identity and the Nation State: The political sociology of multi-cultural societies', *Social Identities*, Vol. 1, No. 1, pp. 21–34.

Rex, John (1997), 'Political Sociology and Cultural Studies in the Study of Migrant Communities in Europe', paper to Conference on Pluralisme culturale, metissage et identita miste, Florence, November.

Rex, J. and Drury, B. (1994), *Ethnic Mobilisation in a Multi-cultural Europe*, Aldershot: Avebury.

Rex, J., Joly, D. and Wilpert, C. (1987), *Immigrant Associations in Europe*, Aldershot: Avebury.

Rex, J. and Moore, R. (1967), *Race, Community and Conflict: A study of Sparkbrook*, London: OUP.

Rex, J. and Tomlinson, S. (1979), *Colonial Immigrant in a British city: A class analysis*, London: Routledge.

Richmond, A.H. (1988), 'Sociological Theories of International Migration: The case of refugees', *Current Sociology*, 36, 2, pp.7–25.

Richmond, A.H. (1994), *Global Apartheid*, Toronto: Oxford University Press.

Roach, P. (1996), Interview, Birmingham, 16 May, CRER.

Rose, D. (1992), *A Climate of Fear. The Murder of PC Blakelock and the Case of the Tottenham Three*, London: Bloomsbury.

Rose, E.J.B., Deakin, N. et al. (1969), *Colour and Citizenship*, London: IRR.

Rose, P.I. (1981), Conference report, 'Towards a Sociology of Exile: A report on an academic symposium', *IMR*, Vol. 15 (1–2), pp. 8–15.

Rudder, V. de and Goodwin, P. (1993/4), 'Theories et Débat sur le Racisme en Grande-Bretagne', *L'homme et la Société*, Paris: L'Harmattan.

Sahgal, G. and Yuval-Davis, N. (eds) (1992), *Refusing Holy Orders. Women and Fundamentalism in Britain*, London: Virago.

Said, E. (1985), *Orientalism*, Harmondsworth: Penguin.

Said, E. (1993), *Culture and Imperialism*, London: Chatto and Windus.

Samad, Y. (1996), 'The Politics of Islamic Identity among Bangladeshis and Pakistanis in Britain', in T. Ranger, Y. Samad and O. Stuart (eds), *Culture, Identity and Politics: Minorities in Britain*, Avebury: Aldershot.

Scarman, Lord (1981), *The Scarman Report on the Brixton Disorders*, Harmondsworth: Penguin Books.

Schierup, C.-U. (1994), 'Multi-culturalism and Ethnic Mobilisation: Some theoretical considerations', in J. Rex and B. Drury (eds), *Ethnic Mobilisation in a Multicultural Europe*, Aldershot: Avebury.

Shacknove, A.E. (1985), 'Who is a Refugee?', *Ethics*, 95 (January), pp. 274–84.

Shaw, C. (1988), 'Latest Estimates of Ethnic Minority Populations', *Population Trends*, No. 51.

Sherrington, J. and Pijjar, N. (1993), The support needs of tenants suffering racial harassment: findings and recommendations of a research survey.

Sillitoe, K. and Cheltzer, H. (1985), *The West Indian School Leaver*, London: HMSO.

Silverman, J. (1986), *Independent Inquiry into the Handsworth Disturbances*, February.

Simmel, G. (1964), *The Sociology of Georg Simmel*, translated, edited and with an introduction by K.H. Wolff, New York: The Free Press.

Simon-Barouh, I. (1982), 'Minorités en France: Populations originaires des pays de l'Asie du Sud-Est Pluriel', No. 32, pp. 59–71.

Sivanandan, A. (1982), *A Different Hunger. Writings on Black resistance*, London: Pluto.

Sivanandan, A. (1990), 'All that Melts into Air is Solid: The hokum of New Times', *Race and Class*, 25, 112.

Smith, A. (1986), *The Ethnic Origins of Nations*, Oxford: Blackwell.

Smith, A.M. (1994), *New Right Discourse on Race and Sexuality in Britain 1968–1990*, Cambridge: Cambridge University Press.

Smith, D. (1974), *Racial Discrimination in Employment*, London: PEP.

Smith, D. (1981), *Unemployment and Racial Minorities*, London: PEP.

Smith, R. (1999), 'Reflections on Migration, the State and the Construction, Durability and Newness of Transnational Life', in L. Pries (ed.), *Migration and Transnational Social Spaces*, Tyne and Wear: Athenaeum Press, pp. 162–87.

Solomos, J. (1996), *Race and Racism in Britain*, Basingstoke: Macmillan.

Solomos, J. (1999), 'Social Research and the Stephen Lawrence Inquiry', *Sociological Research Online*, 4(1).

Solomos, J. and Back, L. (1994), 'Conceptualising Racisms: Social Theory, Politics and Research', *Sociology*, Vol. 28, No. 1, February pp. 143–61.

Solomos, J. and Back, L. (1995), *Race, Politics and Social Change*, London: Routledge.

Solomos, J. and Back, L. (1996), *Racism and Society*, Basingstoke: Macmillan.

Solomos, J., Findlay, R., Jones, S. and Gilroy, P. (1982), 'The Organic Crisis of British Capitalism and Race: The experience of the seventies', in CCCS, *The Empire Strikes Back: Race and racism in '70s Britain*, Centre for Contemporary Cultural Studies, Hutchinson.

Sooben, P. (1990), *The Origins of the Race Relations Act*, Research Paper in Ethnic Relations, Coventry, CRER, University of Warwick.

Spencer, M. (1990), *1992 and All That. Civil Liberties in the Balance*, The Civil Liberties Trust.

Spivak, G. (1990), *The Post-colonial Critic: Interviews, stratégies, dialogues*, London: Routledge.

St Basil Centre, Annual Report 1990–91.

Stedward, G. (1997), *Agendas, Arenas and Antiracism*, PhD thesis, Department of Politics University of Warwick.

Stirling, M. (1992), 'How many Pupils are being Excluded?', *British Journal of Special Education*, 19, 4, pp. 128–30.

Swann Report (1985).

Tattum, D.P. (1982), *Disruptive Pupils in Schools and Units*, London: John Wiley.

Tattum, D.P. (ed.) (1989), *Disruptive Pupil Management*, London: David Fulton.

The Balsall Heathan (1996), No. 163 March/April.

Touraine, A. (1973), *Production de la Société*, Paris: Seuil.

Touraine, A. (1978), *La Voix et le Régard*, Paris: Seuil.

Touraine, A. (1997), *Powerons – Nous Vivre Ensemble? Egaux et Différents*, Paris: Fayard.

Troyna, B. (1982), 'The Ideological and Policy Response to Black Pupils in British Schools', in A. Harnett (ed.), *The Social Sciences in Education Studies*, Heinemann Education: London pp. 127–43.

Troyna, B. (1987), '"Swann's Song": The origins, ideology and implications of "Education for All"', in T.S. Chivers (ed.), *Race and Culture in Education*, Berkshire: NFER-Nelson.

Troyna, B. and Williams, J. (1985), *Racism, Education and the State: the racialisation of education policy*, Beckenham: Croom Helm.

Verhoeven, M. (1997), 'Les Mutations de l'Ordre Scolaire, Régulation et Socialisation dans Quatre Établissements Contrastés', Academia-Bruylant, Louvain-la-Neuve.

Viard, P. (1984), 'Les Crimes Racistes en France', *Les Temps Modernes*, XXXX, No. 452–4, pp. 1942–5.

Virdee, S. (1995), *Racial Violence and Harassment*, London: Policy Studies Institute.

Wallman, S. (1979), *Ethnicity at Work*, London: Macmillan.

Wallman, S. (1986), 'Ethnicity and the Boundary Process in Context', in J. Rex and D. Mason (eds), *Theories of Race and Ethnic Relations*, Cambridge: Cambridge University Press, pp. 226–65.

Ware, V. (1992), *Beyond the Pale: White women, racism and history*, London: Verso.

Warstock and Billesley (1991–92), Detached Youth Work Project, Youthwise, Annual Report.

Watson, J.L. (1977), *Between Two Cultures*, Oxford: Blackwell.

West Midlands Police (1992), Educational Resources April 1992.

West Midlands Police (1994/5), *Annual Report.*

West Midlands Police (1994/5), *Statistics Supplement.*

West Midlands Police (1995), *1991 Census Profile (Post-reorganisation) Force*, Research and Development, July.

West Midlands Police (1995), *1991 Census Profile (Post-reorganisation)* F Division.

West Midlands Police, Race Relations Policy.

Westwood, S. and Bachu, P. (1988), *Enterprising Women, Ethnicity, Economy and Gender Relations*, London: Routledge.

White, J. (1996), Interview Birmingham, 28 April, Community Safety Shop, Newtown.

Wieviorka, M. (1992), *La France Raciste*, Paris: Seuil.

Wieviorka, M. (1993), *La Démocratic à l'Épreuve*, Paris: La Découverte.

Wieviorka, M. (1994), 'Ethnicity as Action', in J. Rex and B. Drury (eds), *Ethnic Mobilisation in a Multi-cultural Europe*, Aldershot: Avebury, pp. 23–9.

Wieviorka, M. (1997), 'Is It So Difficult to be an Anti-Racist?', in P. Werbner and T. Modood (eds), *Debating Cultural Hybridity*, London and New Jersey: Zed Books, pp. 139–54.

Wilkins, G. (1985), *No Passport to Services, a Report on Local Government and Immigration and Nationality Issues*, JCWI, London.

Willems, H. (1995), 'Right-wing Extremism, Racism or Youth Violence? Explaining Violence against Foreigners in Germany', *New Community*, Vol. 21, No. 4, October.

Williams, J. (1992), *Lick My Boots ... Racism in English Football*, Sir Norman Chester Centre for Football Research.

Williams, P. and Chrisman, L. (eds) (1993), *Colonial Discourse and Post-Colonial Theory: A reader*, London: Harvester Wheatsheaf.

Wirth, L. (1928), *The Ghetto*, Chicago.

Withol de Wenden, C. (1994) ,'Changes in the Franco-Maghrebian Association Movement', in J. Rex and B. Drury (eds), *Ethnic Mobilisation in a Multi-cultural Europe*, Aldershot: Avebury, pp. 106–15.

Witte, R. (1995), 'Racist Violence in Western Europe', *New Community*, Vol. 21, No. 4, October.

Witte, R. (1996), *Racist Violence and the State: A comparative European analysis*, Utrecht.

Wrench, J. (1996), 'Organising the Unorganised: "Race": Poor work and trade unions', in P. Ackers et al (eds), *The New Workplace and Trade Unionism*, London: Routledge.

Wrench, J. and Solomos, J. (eds) (1993), *Racism and Migration in Western Europe*, Oxford: Berg Publishers.

Wyndham Place Trust (1980), *Report: Violence in Britain.*

Yinger, M. (1986), 'Intersecting Strands in the Theorisation of Race and Ethnic Relations', in J. Rex and D. Mason (eds), *Theories of Race and Ethnic Relations*, Cambridge: Cambridge University Press, pp. 1–19.

Young, K. and Connelly (1981), *Ethnic Record Keeping Local Authorities*, Policy Studies Institute.

Young, R. (1990), *White Mythologies: Writing history and the West*, London: Routledge.

Young, R. (1995), *Colonial Desire: Hybridity in theory, culture and race*, London: Routledge.

Youth Justice in Birmingham (1995), 'Promoting Youth Justice and Reducing Offending by Children and Young people', Annual Report 1994/95.

Youth Offender Profile 1993 (1994), Birmingham, June.

Youth Offender Profile, Birmingham 1994, West Midlands Joint Data Team.

Yuval-Davis, N. (1993), 'Gender and Nation', *Ethnic and Racial Studies*, 16, No. 4 October, pp. 621–31.

Zolberg, A.R., Suhrke, A. and Aguayo, S. (1989), *Escape from Violence: Conflict and the refugee crisis in the developing world*, Oxford: Oxford University Press, p. 380.

Zucker, N.L. and Zucker, N.F. (1987), *The Guarded Gate: the reality of American refugee policy*, San Diego: Harcourt Brace Jovanovich.